A Harvest of
Hawai'i Plantation Pidgin
The Japanese Way

Myra Sachiko Ikeda

Illustrations by

Jeffery Kalehuakea DeCosta

with a Foreword by

Arnold Hiura

Mutual Publishing

ISBN-13: 978-1939487-58-2
Library of Congress Control Number: 2015951898
Design by Jane Gillespie
Cover images: (top) © Tabitazn|Dreamstime.com;
(center) © Exopixel|Dreamstime.com; (bottom) ©
MattySymmons|Dreamstime.com

First Printing, January 2016
Second Printing, November 2016

Mutual Publishing, LLC
1215 Center Street, Suite 210
Honolulu, Hawaii 96816
Ph: (808) 732-1709
Fax: (808) 734-4094
e-mail: info@mutualpublishing.com
www.mutualpublishing.com

Printed in South Korea

Contents

Foreword

by Arnold Hiura

There was a time in the not-too-distant past when driving around any of the Hawaiian Islands meant cruising miles of rural roads flanked by fields of waving sugar cane.

The curtain of cane would occasionally part to reveal quaint plantation towns—some so small that you'd miss them if you blinked. Others, much more substantial, might include a post office, school, general store, gas station, barbershop, theater and churches of various religious faiths.

The seemingly endless acres of sugar cane and small plantation towns are almost all gone now, replaced by other agricultural enterprises, modern housing developments, and strip malls. Mom-and-pop stores have given way to mini marts, self-serve gas stations, and big chain convenience stores.

"So what?" you might ask. "Isn't this simply progress taking its course?" While this may be true, it would be a shame for Hawai'i's plantations to be treated like obscure artifacts left on the side of the road without any appreciation of how they helped shape what Hawai'i is today.

After all, sugar (and also pineapple) plantations served as guideposts to Hawai'i's development for over a century. Tens of thousands of immigrants arrived from China, Korea, Portugal, Puerto Rico, the Philippines, Japan and in smaller numbers from other countries to work on Hawai'i's plantations. Many settled here and, collectively, they and their offspring helped to transform island society.

Thanks in part to its host culture, combined with other factors, Hawai'i somehow provided an environment where different ethnic groups were able to retain important aspects of their cultural heritage while forging a shared multiethnic identity. Food, clothing and language were some of the key components that were artfully muddled into this rich cultural cocktail. Some aspects of a person's culture were specifically relegated to the privacy of one's home or ethnic community while others were shared publicly with the community at large. People freely exercised their religious beliefs, ceremonies, and festive traditions, which were accepted and even embraced by others, adding layers of diversity to plantation life.

Indeed, these outwardly sleepy plantation towns moved to their own beat, with all residents participating in synch with one another. The mill whistle roused everyone out of bed at dawn. Workers assembled at the labor yard, and children reported to school. In the afternoon, kids spilled out from classrooms and onto playgrounds that erupted into the cacophony of kids at play. Local sports teams practiced on ball fields and in gymnasiums. The general store was abuzz with small talk, and others tended to their vegetable gardens before retreating home ahead of the setting sun to partake of simple, satisfying meals, such as rice, hot tea, and pickled vegetables.

Over time, plantation camps came to make as great or even greater an imprint on a person's identity than his or her ethnic background—especially as second and third generation children were born to plantation workers and intermarriage between ethnic groups grew more and more commonplace. Together, residents celebrated weddings, the birth of children, and mourned the passing of relatives, neighbors and friends.

In *A Harvest of Hawai'i Plantation Pidgin: The Japanese Way*, Myra Sachiko Ikeda explores the important role that Pidgin English played in the dynamics of this evolving local identity. This is a challenging task, to say the least, but only through the process of documentation will this history ever be preserved, shared and appreciated.

Even in focusing specifically on Japanese Pidgin, there are just too many words and variations in the language for anyone to record them all in a single collection. Adding to the immensity of the challenge is the fact that words sometimes varied from island to island and, in some cases, even from district to district. Perhaps one of Ikeda's most extreme examples of this characteristic is the game called *kamapio*, which not only varied in spelling and pronunciation, but was even played by different rules from town to town.

Moreover, in *A Harvest of Hawai'i Plantation Pidgin,* Ikeda does more than merely list words, sharing her personal story and motivation in tackling this project. Through diligence and years of hard work, she has given others more than just a starting point, but a valuable framework through which they might understand, organize, and otherwise add or modify terms as their own experience dictates.

Finally, as Ikeda points out in her book, one did not have to live on a plantation for his or her life to be enriched by Plantation Pidgin. For the most part, towns—especially on the Neighbor Islands—existed largely to serve the plantation workers and could indeed be considered extensions of the plantation.

Today, even in its most contemporary form, Hawai'i folks still recognize even the slightest hint of Pidgin being spoken by others, no matter what the context. While traveling away from the islands, for example—in an airport terminal, hotel lobby, or restaurant—anyone from Hawaiʻi will immediately recognize and locate the source of a Pidgin-sounding voice. "Where you from?" they might ask. "What school you grad?" And, before long, conversation finds its way back to one's *hanabata* days…

Ahhh. "Hanabata Days," in fact, may very well be the perfect Japanese Pidgin term, for not only does it combine Japanese *hana* (nose) with English *bata* (butter), but it also forms a phrase that whisks all of us back to our childhood, to a time when some of us might recall growing up as snot-nosed kids on a plantation, oblivious to the crunch of unpaved gravel roads beneath our bare feet (*hadashi*).

More importantly, "Hanabata Days" was a time when we learned how to get along with others whose lives may be quite different than ours, but instinctually knew how to establish common ground, as in the case with language. Plantation Pidgin and the values that it taught us were simply part of a way of life… one that may be gone, but should not be allowed to fade from our memories.

Preface

Many aspects of life in the plantation camps and in the communities were accepted and never questioned regardless of their outward differences. The identical houses of the workers in the camps were lined up like "pretty maids all in a row." The managers' homes, on the other hand, were usually large and elegant with expansive sprawling lawns. They were even sometimes nestled on a rise. In comparison to the "pretty maids all in a row," these homes stood out like the "King of the Hill."

There were other aspects of life, however, in which differences were not simply just accepted but overcome. Overcoming these differences was instrumental toward forging the bonds among the various ethnic groups who lived on the plantations. From these bonds was born a common understood language which was critical for without it plantation work could not be accomplished. It is the impact this language had on Japanese and the assimilation of lifestyles and cultures from which it developed that is the subject of this book.

Acknowledgments

A deep appreciation to everyone who shared their stories, thoughts, concepts and insights with me on this journey. Your sharing has been truly vital to this book.

I apologize for any misinterpretations, mistakes and other misses for they are truly of my own doing.

✻ ✠ ✻

Introduction

This book began circa 1976 as a project in college about the Japanese language used as I was growing up. The intent was to educate myself about the development and change of the Japanese language within the sugar cane plantation communities particularly on Hawai'i Island as it was initially influenced by and eventually became a part of Pidgin English. The introspective role this project has undertaken since its inception is gratifying. I am indebted to those who encouraged me to share the combined knowledge, experiences and memories of the people I spoke with at the onset of the project and those with whom I met more recently on this journey. This sharing has now become particularly imminent with the passing of the generations. I am humbled and grateful to the many who shared the bonds of plantation life for their inspiration and support.

While the journey has been indeed a heartwarming one, it has also been a reality check for me. I realized since the mid-1970s when I first thought about this subject and putting thoughts to paper now, almost four decades later, that I am not really that same person. Nor should I be. Yes, I may still have the same heart, passion and commitment but the years have perhaps given me a sensibility and sensitivity which only time can bring. And while I can revisit, I cannot really go home again…and neither could my book. Should it have been written forty years ago, it might have been more focused on the framework of the dynamics in the changes of languages when they develop in isolated areas away from their original country. While it is a phenomenon which no doubt may be significant and fascinating, it is now not the focus of this book.

Rather, this book is about the journey many have taken during their days of plantation life. It is to express the nostalgia of their experiences as well as my own; and to share the Japanese contribution to this life. During my "talk story" with people, we always found ourselves walking down memory lane reminiscing of how things were "back in the good old days." The laughter and memories of those times which have now passed warmed our hearts. We always had, too, the gratitude and respect for our ancestors as they struggled to survive and to make our lives better. It is my wish to share these wonderful feelings, if even for a moment, of this era passed.

I remember as I was growing up that my father was the breadwinner who went to work to ensure that the family's needs were met. My mother was the housewife who made sure the home was a sanctuary which we could retreat to at any time. It was she who served as my inspiration in learning about and embracing the Japanese language and culture. After all, her honor and celebration of the culture and traditions of our ethnic background, a country I often heard referred to as "the homeland" or "mother country" of Japan, was contagious. Her enthusiasm for anything Japanese was not unlike many others who felt that special connection to Japan even if they lived in Hawai'i their entire lives. She was a mother who truly raised her child in the tradition of *kodomo no tameni* - for the sake of the children. Throughout her life, she talked about things Japanese and made sure I had the opportunities to see and to participate in whatever Hawai'i offered of the Japanese culture.

I attended Japanese language school for twelve years not even missing those days I didn't attend English school (refers to public school where the curriculum was taught in English and is used as a differentiation from Japanese school), took three years of Japanese in high school, another four in college and finally majored in Japanese Studies. I learned *ikebana* (flower arrangement) weekly for six years and even studied *chanoyu* (tea ceremony) classes during my college years. I participated in the *bon* dances (dances held as part of the religious observance to honor one's ancestors) ever since I could walk. In 1977, I married another *sansei* (third generation of Japanese descent) who further inspired me to understand and experience Japanese society and its ways.

The apple does not fall far from the tree because like my mom I, too, wanted to share whatever knowledge I had about the Japanese language and culture. I did this through teaching opportunities with the Japanese Chamber of Commerce & Industry of Hawaiʻi; the Hawaiʻi Community College Office of Continuing Education & Training; the University of Hawaiʻi at Hilo Conference Center; the Hawaiʻi State Department of Education; University of Hawaiʻi at Manoa's Okinawan Dance Course; Jimpu Kai Kin Ryosho Ryukyu Geino Kenkyusho, Hawaiʻi Shibu and through other on-site cultural demonstrations and lessons.

As mentioned earlier, I started this project while in college and referred to it as "the development of the Japanese language in the sugar plantation communities." Although I did not live on a sugar plantation per se, the plantations infused all parts of life. Just by virtue of living in communities where they were located, the plantation lifestyle, its culture and language included, was part of your lifestyle. So it was that how people spoke on the plantation was how people spoke in the community—plantation talk was community talk.

A single word, *erai*, was the catalyst for this project. Throughout all the years of growing up, *erai* meant one thing and one thing only, "tired." Imagine my shock when I learned *erai* in standard Japanese was defined as "great" and even "excellent, admirable, remarkable, distinguished…" I do not find myself speechless too often but, I must admit, this was definitely one of those moments. It was then I thought if the Hawai'i meaning of *erai* can be so different from the Japanese meaning, what other words and phrases are out there? What do we use in Hawai'i which do not have the same meaning in Japan? With writing instrument in hand and with whatever paper I could write on, I began on a mission to find them. The first resource was me since I was the most accessible. My next resources were my mom followed by some friends and then others, all who had grown up during the time when sugar was king. After graduating college in 1978, I took my little plaid spiral notebook in which I came to gather my wordly treasures and put it on a shelf where it sat. The shelf moved as I moved and the book moved, too, sitting patiently on the shelf until such a day it would once again record the legacy of the past.

My mom, meanwhile, passed away on June 5, 2006, having never set foot on the land she always dreamed about. Her death, exactly two months after my fiftieth birthday, made me realize that we must make every effort to accomplish our dreams and desires while we are still able to achieve them. I guess my book must have thought that, too, because one day when I sat down to ponder my future, it called to me. I looked at it but didn't pay it any attention. A little while later it called a little louder and then finally it yelled at me. It was now time to continue on the mission. The goal of thirty-seven years ago had now turned into an item on my bucket list. So once again I am continuing on with my journey.

Yes, this project certainly has been a journey, one with many, many paths. Each path is as fascinating as another so I am truly amazed, and grateful, to be able to actually complete some part of this journey long enough to write about it. As I look upon the paths of this journey, I am reminded of "The Road Not Taken" by Robert Frost.

> *"Two roads diverged in a yellow wood,*
> *And sorry I could not travel both*
> *And be one traveler, long I stood…*
> *I took the one less traveled by,*
> *And that has made all the difference."*

For with each path chosen, there were others left untaken. The people I met, whether by planned design, through an introduction or serendipitously, have all been incredible and each has played an important role as they accompanied me on various parts of my journey.

Through this book I would like to honor each generation for its important role in contributing to the culture and language of Hawai'i. The *issei* (first generation of Japanese descent—the Japanese immigrants) who planted the seeds which future generations would harvest. The *nisei* (second generation of Japanese descent—children of the *issei*) who were unwittingly caught between the struggles of two countries and two cultures. Their experiences were crucial in guiding and inspiring their children and following generations. The *sansei* (third generation of Japanese descent) who witnessed the passing of the culture and language born on the sugar cane plantations as they saw the passing of their parents and grandparents. They now honor the legacy of their ancestors and the memories of an era past by passing on the bounty of the preceding generations to their *yonsei* (fourth generation of Japanese descent) children, *gosei* (fifth generation of Japanese descent) grandchildren and to future generations.

Since I make categorical distinctions between each generation, I should like to offer here an explanation as to why. I believe the thought processes, beliefs and practices are often influenced by the hierarchy of the generations rather than by actual age. That is to say, someone in their 80s may think more like someone in their 50s rather than someone in their 70s although the person in their 70s is closer in age to the person in their 80s. The reason is because the person in their 50s and the person in their 80s are both of the same *sansei* generation. The *nisei* still carry with them a strong influence from their *issei* parents whereas the *sansei* have already been buffered from this influence by their *nisei* parents. This closeness of age of some *sansei* to the age of some *nisei* is due to the span of time during which immigrants came to Hawai'i. The *issei* came to Hawai'i over several decades and hence, the child of an immigrant who came in the 1800s would be considered a *nisei* as well as the child of an immigrant who came during 1910s—1920s but they would be of vastly different ages. While this age differential can result in some *sansei* actually being closer in age to the *nisei* parents of their *sansei* counterparts, their way of thinking tends not to be.

Let us now continue the journey back to when the Japanese came to work on the sugar cane plantations with the intent on returning home at the end of their contract period.

✻ ✤ ✻

CHAPTER 1

Legacy of the Dream

This journey did not really begin with me but rather with the dreams of the thousands of Japanese who seized the opportunity to come to Hawai'i hoping to seek their fortunes by working for a few years on the sugar cane plantations and returning home to Japan to live prosperously. Unfortunately for many, these dreams of accumulated wealth would never be fulfilled and they would never return to Japan. These dreams for which they toiled so hard would become just a sliver of hope. Their legacy, however, lives on as they and their future generations remain in Hawai'i. Their culture rich in values, traditions and arts would be carried on by their succeeding generations and eventually become part of the fabric which is Hawai'i.

These values were fundamental in helping the immigrants survive and succeed in a foreign land many would eventually call home. Instilled for centuries into the Japanese, they were passed on by the *issei* to future generations. Some of these are: *giri*, sense of duty and honor; *on*, debt of gratitude; *oyakōkō*, filial piety; *gaman*, perseverance; *ganbari*, endurance; *shikataganai*, resigned acceptance of a situation because it can't be helped but be that way; *sekinin*, responsibility; *haji*, shame; *kansha*, gratitude; *chūgi*, loyalty and devotion; *eiyo* honor; and *gisei*, sacrifice. The importance of

these values as characteristics of the Japanese are encompassed in the term, *Yamato-damashī* which was coined to describe the spirit reflecting the native values of the Japanese, differentiating them from the values of foreign nations. It is ironic that this spirit of Japan passed on by the *issei* parents to their *nisei* children is what made many Hawai'i soldiers outstanding as they fought Japan during World War II.

Just as the values were important in the immigrants' survival in a new land, communication with their multiethnic counterparts with whom they worked was essential. By the time the Japanese arrived, the Hawaiian, Chinese and Portuguese languages seemed to have already formed the basis of the common language, Pidgin English. (In linguistics, Pidgin refers to a new language that develops because of the need to communicate by speakers who do not share a common language. Pidgin English indicates that English is the primary language on which it is based.) However, the contribution of other ethnic groups such as the Japanese to this language should not be overlooked. As with other ethnic groups, the dialects brought by the Japanese contributed to and blended together with the languages and dialects of each ethnic group working on the sugar cane plantations ultimately resulting in a language unique to Hawai'i. Fondly referred to in Hawai'i as Pidgin, the language developed out of the desire for people to communicate with one another and represents the bonds of interconnectivity that people feel with each other. Pidgin is the language which identifies Hawai'i as it reflects the shared knowledge and experiences of its peoples.

Scholars, researchers, those writing memoirs and everyone in between and beyond have written articles, theses, books and tomes on Japanese immigration through life on the plantation and Pidgin English. It is not my intent or inclination to repeat these writings or to make any judgments. The focus here is on the development of Pidgin English, particularly of the Japanese language in the sugar cane plantation communities primarily on Hawai'i Island. I like to call this language Hawai'i Plantation Pidgin. The primary focus of this book is the development and change in the language but its evolution within the broader spectrum of the Hawai'i Plantation Pidgin culture will also be discussed.

As part of the continuum of language development and evolution, this language developed at varying stages into Hawai'i Creole English. The demise of the language spoken on the plantation can be attributed to, I believe, two primary reasons. Firstly, those who spoke it have passed on or are passing on. Secondly, Hawai'i Plantation Pidgin is being superseded by both Standard English and Hawai'i Creole English. The succeeding generations have either slowly forgotten the language which has come to be no longer used or were never aware of it. When I asked those with whom I spoke as to how they communicated during the plantation days, without hesitation, they replied they spoke Pidgin but most couldn't recall specific words or phrases without the benefit of an actual conversation. While I refer to this language of the past as Hawai'i Plantation Pidgin, it really wasn't unique only to the plantation but was spoken by the whole community because the plantation was such an integral part of the community. I would like to harvest and share the bounty from these seeds of Hawai'i Plantation Pidgin which our ancestors planted because this is part of their legacy and it is part of our legacy.

This legacy essentially began in 1868 when the *gannen mono* (first year people) of the Meiji Era, 1868-1912, immigrated to Hawai'i aboard the British ship HMS *Scioto* as a result of King Kamehameha IV's request in 1860 to the Japanese government to consider a Treaty of Friendship. It was an understanding that this treaty was a temporary agreement to begin the recruitment of sugar plantation laborers. The number of immigrants aboard the HMS *Scioto* varied among the sources I researched, numbering from one hundred forty-seven to one hundred fifty-three. This variance could reflect how the immigrants were counted such as whether this number reflected only the laborers themselves or if children were included as well. During this journey, it was recorded that one man passed away and a baby boy, Yotaro, was born. Interestingly, the emigration itself was actually illegal since the Meiji Government had refused its authorization.

Reasons for recruiting sugar plantation laborers were mutually beneficial to both the Japanese and Hawaiian governments. Japan was going through transition during the 1870s and 1880s. The Meiji government needed to somehow reduce the tensions caused by various changes that resulted in a bleak and prolonged depression. This new government had to provide compensation to the entire *samurai* (warrior, especially military retainers of *daimyo*, Japanese feudal lord, in the Edo or Tokugawa period, 1803–1868) class since it took over exclusive rights to political military power. The changes in tax laws caused rice prices to fall almost fifty percent within three years causing massive devastation to the villages throughout the countryside. Many were trying to avoid the new military conscription. The emigration of its citizens to Hawai'i seemed a viable way to lessen the problems of unemployment, political chaos and rioting. The Meiji government also saw this as a way to gain knowledge of modern agricultural techniques that the emigrants would be sure to bring with them when they returned home. Additionally, it sought the foreign capital which would be sent home by workers overseas. In fact, it happened that the monies sent by the immigrants back to Japan during the Meiji Period did amount annually to more than 2 million yen (Japan's present currency system which was established in 1871), approximately the equivalent of $1 million U.S. dollars (based on 1 yen = 50 cents in U.S. dollars). "The Hiroshima Prefecture Statistical Annals" show that a laborer sent back an average of 70 yen in 1898 compared with a laborer in 1910 who sent back about 175 yen. The Annals further show that immigrants returning to Hiroshima in 1908 brought back an average of 800 yen per person.

Many of the immigrants themselves had personal reasons for seeking employment outside of their homeland. One was the custom of primogeniture—the birthright of the eldest son to inherit his parents' land. This custom dictated that no property was left for the younger sons leaving them to seek employment elsewhere. Another reason was to earn money. Many hoped to be able to escape the life of poverty and to create a better life for their children as well as themselves. For others, it was not only the desire to earn enough money for bettering their lives but it was to earn their fortune so they may return home as wealthy respected men. In one case, for instance, the possibility of earning 212 yen in Hawai'i compared with only 10 yen a year in Japan was too appealing. There were others who wished to escape the rigidity of Japan's social classes by starting a new life and, possibly, become affluent in the process. For many, it was better being a stranger in a strange land rather than facing the shame as a failure in their homeland. Still yet, another reason was simply the love of adventure.

In Hawai'i, the realization that industrial sugar production required intensive manpower caused plantation owners to seek workers outside of Hawai'i. The original labor force of native Hawaiians was drastically reduced due to the ravaging diseases brought by foreigners. Furthermore, the Hawaiians who were accustomed to working for their chiefs had difficulty in adjusting to the labor intensive work on a ten to twelve hour shift daily working for a foreigner particularly when they could easily subsist by farming and fishing.

The hope of the Japanese to leave their suffering amidst the economic and political chaos of their country for a better life in Hawai'i; and the need of the plantation owners to look outside of Hawai'i to fill their workforce seemed to be a synergistic relationship that would fulfill the needs of both countries.

CHAPTER 2

The Beginnings of Hawaiʻi Plantation Pidgin

The virtue in the hearts of the people from different cultures and lifestyles as they genuinely tried to communicate with one another is reflected in the purity of Hawaiʻi Plantation Pidgin. These words and phrases were simply what made up the language, their origins were unimportant. Those with whom I spoke made no distinction, and often could not and did not recognize the different originating language or languages of words or phrases. Nor did they care. The importance was that this language, Hawaiʻi Plantation Pidgin, allowed people to effectively communicate with each other. With no judgment of what was right or wrong and with no outside stimuli, the language evolved within itself. It was only natural that all the spoken languages of the plantation become its own language. Basically, each camp was its own community closed off to the rest of the world with no information flowing in or out. Each camp in a way, you might say, had its own dialect. It was only when someone went away or came into contact with people with whom they did not normally associate did they became aware of the existence of different words or ideas. As a result, the fluidity and constant development of Hawaiʻi Plantation Pidgin itself grew as the intermingling of

Kohala Sugar Mill ca: 1890

people of different backgrounds and of different camps increased and the need to communicate about more things, newer things and different things increased as well.

Perhaps Hawai'i Plantation Pidgin could have simply begun as two people, each within their own framework, talking to each other with each person trying to best transmit their information to the next person. As more pairs and groups of people continued this method of communication, perhaps the code of their individual languages expanded into the mainstream itself resulting finally into a language of widespread use. Of course, this thought is simply my own conjecture and is in no way meant to be a statement of fact.

The importance of Hawai'i Plantation Pidgin's origin cannot be overlooked. It developed as a language whose purpose was to allow people to verbally communicate in a common language. Therefore, as a spoken and not a written language, the spelling of many words can be wide and varied. For instance, "by and by" contracted to, pronounced and often spelled *bambai* is also spelled in numerous other ways such as *bumbai, bumby* or *bum by*, and *bumbye* or *bum bye* as well as *bumbi* and *bumbbi*.

While there can be many ways to spell a word, there are also many words to describe one thing as well. For instance, "to bathe" can be *'au'au, wai wai, bocha* or *jabu*.

A common thought shared by many of the people I spoke with was that many words and phrases were shortened or somehow contracted from their standard or original form. Were these contractions part of the effort in trying to speak quickly? Everyone was supposed to be working and would suffer grave negative consequences should they be caught loafing under the watchful eye of the *luna* (foreman; boss; leader; overseer; supervisor). Would taking a shorter time to communicate avoid this punishment? Would using words rather than complete sentences and speaking quickly take a shorter amount of time away from their work? Could the consideration of time also be a reason for such directness of the language? As there was no time to waste, political correctness was not a priority. The message needed to be delivered as quickly and directly in the shortest time possible.

Perhaps this rapid speech unintentionally played a role in creating new words—faster speech resulted in changing the pronunciation of the original words. For example, *pa'akikī* meaning stubborn or hard has been shortened to *pakiki* by eliminating the following: (1) the short pause after the first a, (2) the second a and (3) the elongated sound of the second i.

This rapid speech may still be continuing in today's speech as well for it has often been observed by non-Pidgin speakers that Hawai'i people speak quickly. It's no wonder with the combination of rapid speech, diverse word origins, creative pronunciations and wordsmithing that Hawai'i Plantation Pidgin and its successor languages are difficult to understand by those who didn't speak it during any time in their lives.

A recurring question for me was the time period during which Hawai'i Plantation Pidgin was spoken. From the establishment of Kohala Sugar Company in 1863 until the closing of Ka'ū Sugar Company in 1996, plantation life spanned over a hundred and thirty years on Hawai'i Island. However, since the first Japanese immigration occurred only five years after the first plantation was established, the time period of focusing on the Japanese language still essentially reflects the entire span of the sugar industry's existence on the island. One qualifier as to what I would consider Hawai'i Plantation Pidgin is if I thought my *obāchan* (grandmother) would understand what is being said. For instance, I believe, she would understand what is meant by *chawan cut* (a haircut which looks like it resulted from a rice bowl being placed upside down on the head). On the other hand, I don't think she would understand *garans ballbarans* or even *garans*, both words meaning "guaranteed." Nor do I believe she would understand the word *choke* to mean "plenty." She passed away when I was in kindergarten and, like the other *issei*, is no longer here to say yea or nay to my judgment. As mentioned in the introduction, I want to address the language and the culture as I was growing up so I am trying to be mindful of both *obāchan* and myself as I write this book.

One challenging issue I encountered in expressing the language and culture of our ancestors, and the subject of interesting if not controversial discussions, was how words of certain subject matter could be put forth in a non-offensive way. Of particular concern was words used for ethnic groups because the sensitivity of racial overtones is higher today than in an era past. People of the plantation knew there was segregation between the whites and the color. The whites, after all, had the better jobs and lived on the other side of town. Yes, there were camps of the various ethnic groups such as the Hawaiians, Chinese, Portuguese, Japanese, Puerto Ricans, Filipinos and Koreans. But within the camps themselves, the members didn't feel segregation existed perhaps because everyone was a laborer. It was on this common bond on which they focused and not their differences. Whether this was an unconsciously-, a subconsciously- or consciously-made decision doesn't matter because it was an accepted part of plantation life. Everyone took part in each other's celebrations and adversities assisting whatever way possible without thought to the camp in which someone lived. They were your friends so you went to support and honor them because that's what friends do. The culture of respect for all ethnic groups was a way of life.

There is a multiplicity of words used to describe ethnic groups in the form of characteristics attributed to the particular ethnic group. One viewpoint may be that physical and character traits often led to terms which people thought were descriptive of them. While these people may not have been of the ethnic group being described, I believe both in my experiences and in talking with others about their experiences, that these terms were used as descriptors and had no negative connotations. Another viewpoint to consider is that since each camp was essentially its own community, its members simply accepted what they were told. This viewpoint is in tandem with much of Hawaiʻi Plantation Pidgin itself where the importance was the ability to communicate with each other and not the origins of the words. Additionally, children were raised in a "children should be seen and not heard" environment where you dare not question what you were told. A *sansei* put it succinctly when he said, "Whatever we were told was what we used, we didn't know any better." That is to say, it is important to keep in mind that the context within the framework of how we are introduced to certain words and how their meaning is conveyed as we learn them plays a vital role in how they are used. If a word was learned simply as a description, the word was accepted as such with none of the nuances it may have originally had attached to it.

Some of these terms were even included as part of daily life such as in children's games and nursery rhymes. For example, the following jingle honors the financial acumen of the Chinese:

> *Ching Chong Chinaman*
> *Sitting on the fence*
> *Trying to made a dollar*
> *Out of fifteen cents.*

Then there is the word "Jap," a contraction for "Japanese." While it could be construed as a racist term, when looked at within the context of the military culture where abbreviations to shorten words or phrases is common, it doesn't seem as derogatory as one's initial reaction may purport it to be. As with the rapid speech of Hawai'i Plantation Pidgin in order to avoid incurring the wrath of the *luna*, in the military a second in combat can mean life or death, literally. For instance saying, "I saw Japs three klicks north" (klick being the military term for metric measurement) is much more efficient and less time-consuming than saying, "I saw approximately five Japanese soldiers about a mile and a half at the 12 o'clock position." Another case-in-point regarding military abbreviations is that they call their eating area "dfac" (pronounced "d" for the letter d and "fac" as in factory), an abbreviation of "dining facility."

Regardless of what we may think today, the words, offensive or otherwise, were a real part of communication in the plantation.

[CHAPTER 3]

Camp Names

Housing in the form of grass huts were provided by the Hawaiian government for most of the sugar industry's original workforce of native Hawaiians. As the sugar industry grew, the plantations began importing laborers from various countries and provided their contracted laborers with free housing. The recruitment of this multiethnic workforce may have been for economic or political purposes such as to avoid any particular group becoming dominant or to separate groups as a means to increase production. It has also been said that the plantation placed people in certain areas to make for an easier transition. The placement of these laborers by ethnic groups may have provided for ease of communication and for morale. After all, keeping members of the same ethnic group together probably made for a stronger sense of community, continuity and cultural identity. While this placement may have been carefully orchestrated, it may also have been a matter of simple timing due to the different periods of arrival by the various ethnic groups.

It appears for the Japanese that they may have within their own community identified themselves as being from different prefectures. This is reflected in their different *hōgen* (dialects) such as Hiroshima-ben, Yamaguchi-ben and Kumamoto-ben

which have all contributed to Hawai'i Plantation Pidgin. Although from a non-Japanese perspective, they were all probably viewed homogeneously as Japanese.

Plantations on Hawai'i Island used the term "camps" on their maps to explain where their employees lived. Accordingly, I am following their lead and using that term here. The set-up and arrangement of these camps seem to have been born out of practical considerations. For example, as the mill was a focal point for the plantations building the camps around it was logical. The workers needed to be in close proximity to the fields in which they worked. They had to walk since there were no vehicles to transport them so locating camps close to the fields in which they labored was practical.

Since camp names give such an insight to the multi-faceted perspectives that went into naming them, I feel not including them here would be remiss on my part. For instance, segregation by ethnicity in the plantation camps was common and originally many camps were referred to by ethnic names. There was Japanese Camp in Keaʻau (formerly ʻOlaʻa, home to Puna Sugar) and Onomea and Japanese Mill Camp in Pahala; Portuguese Camp in Keaʻau, Kohala and Onomea; Podagee Camp in Pahala; Filipino Camp in Keaʻau and Onomea and Filipino Mill Camp in Pahala; Korean Camp in Pahala and Hāmākua, Korean Camp aka Wainaku Camp 2 in Hilo; Chinese Camp or Pake Camp in Hāmākua; Hawaiian Camp in Kohala; and Puerto Rican Camp in Keaʻau and Hāmākua.

Camps were also known by their close proximity to a prominent place. Often, the prominent place in the plantation was its store and Store Camp was naturally in its immediate vicinity as in Keaʻau. Store Camp was also located in the area of Nakahara Store in Hāmākua. Of course, sometimes a camp was not simply called Store Camp because of its location near the store but would be known according to the name of the store such as Chong Camp in Pahala or by the name of the family who ran the store such as Otake Camp in Waialua on the Island of Oʻahu. Another prominent place in the plantation was its stable and located in Pāpaʻaloa was Stable Camp. There was a plantation gym in Niu Village situated north of Hilo where Gym Camp was located. Of course, one cannot forget the importance of the mill, and hence, Mill Camp was located in the back of ʻŌʻōkala Mill and yet another Mill Camp could be found around the mill in Waialua. In Waialua, there was Lua (toilet; outhouse; bathroom) Camp which got its name because of the reservoir there. It is interesting to note here that although each camp was essentially a contained unit, the mishearing, mispronunciation and misunderstanding of words and names also occurred within those living in the camps as well. No outside influence was needed for that. For instance, Lua Camp was known as Lower Camp to some who lived in Waialua.

Camps were also named according to their location in a particular geographical area. This method was used by the Laupāhoehoe Sugar Company in naming the following camps: Kaiaʻakea Camp in Kaiaʻakea, Maulua Camp in Maulua, Kapehu Camp in Kapehu, Kekoa Camp in an area in Pāpaʻaloa, Kilau Camp in Laupāhoehoe Mauka (Kilau was a small area along the gulch in Laupāhoehoe Mauka) and Waipunalei Camp, an area on the top and Honokaa side of Laupāhoehoe Point which served as the end point for the Laupāhoehoe Sugar camps.

A determined distance from a geographical locale was another approach in naming camps. There are some camps in Keaʻau, for example, named according to their distance from Hilo where you can find 8-Mile Camp, 8 and a half-mile camp aka "8-mile half Camp" and 9-mile Camp.

A popular way of naming camps was by naming them after a boss, supervisor or *luna*. Iwasaki Camp in Kurtistown was named after labor contractor, Jirokichi Iwasaki, the first person to be hired for the ʻOlaʻa reclamation project. In Pāhala, there was Higashi Camp in Maula, Kai Camp in Kapapala and Kusumoto Camp in Maia. Kaiwiki Sugar Company used bosses for their camp names. These included Quintana Camp, Machida Camp, Salvino Camp or Florentino Camp, Ah Ching Camp also known as Chinese or Pake Camp, Kishi Camp or Sato Camp, Belaski Camp, Akasaki Camp, Fujiyoshi or Pulapula (seedlings, sprouts, cuttings, as of sugar cane) Camp, Ramon Camp, Segundo Fernando Camp, Hashimura Camp, Uchida Camp and Ishikawa Camp.

Numbers also served as a basis for camp names. In Kaʻu, Camp 1 and Camp 2 could be found. In Pāhoa, the camps were numbered one through six. Also numbered but specific to a particular location were Wainaku Camp 1 and Wainaku Camp 2.

Camps often took on the name for what they were known. For instance, since the baseball team at 9-mile Camp in Keaʻau was called the Blues, the camp came to be known as Blues Camp. In Pāhala, because the pre-fab houses came from Olokele, Kauaʻi, the camp was called Olokele. Kukui Village in ʻŌʻōkala got its name because of a large *kukui* (*Aleurites moluccana*) tree at its entrance. The hall located here was used by families for social gatherings and community use. A camp in Puʻunene on Maui was known as Pump Camp because a large pump that ran twenty-four hours a day was in its midst. This camp was later renamed with a number.

Chronology served yet as another way of naming camps. There was Shin (New) Camp in Keaʻau which signified new development, New Camp in Kohala and New Hawaiian Camp in Pāhala.

The distinction between management and workers was also reflected in camp names. In Hāmākua, the *luna* lived in Skilled Camp and in Waialua, the supervisors lived in Ranch Camp.

As one can see, camp names were not necessarily given indiscriminately but rather by taking into account thoughtful consideration of various viewpoints.

CHAPTER 4

Frozen in Time

Many Japanese never returned home at the end of their contract period as planned. Therefore, a few decades passed before they actually established themselves as part of their new homeland. Despite the fact their culture and language had changed during their life on the plantations, they clung steadfastly to their identity as being Japanese. Although the *issei* and *nisei* were no longer part of their native homeland, they continued to identify themselves as Japanese, no different from the Japanese in Japan. Just as the Japanese in Japan, they used the term *gaijin* (foreigner) to identify any non-Japanese albeit they had essentially become *gaijin* themselves when viewed from the Japanese perspective.

This strong identity which tied them to the homeland they left and being isolated in the expanse of the Pacific Ocean were important contributing factors to what is often referred to as a "frozen culture." In other words, Hawaii's Japanese culture and language can be attributed to being frozen in time of the Meiji Era. This should not be surprising if one considers that approximately 138,000 Japanese immigrated to Hawai'i from the arrival the *gannen mono* in 1868 through 1907.

All but a memory in Japan, the life of the Meiji Era thrived in Hawai'i. While its echoes still may be found here today even these echoes have now grown softer. This preservation, I believe, was an important contribution in the development of Hawai'i Plantation Pidgin. Similar to the camps receiving no outside influences, the language of the Meiji Era was able to survive in Hawai'i because there were no outside stimuli to change it and as a result it played an important role in Hawai'i Plantation Pidgin—The Japanese Way.

For me, the reality of being frozen in this time period came to light while visiting a relative in Japan during the early 1980s. She had this absolutely astonished look on her face when I mentioned *hinoshi* (iron, as in ironing clothes). I probably had an equally astonished look when I saw her expression. I wondered why using a Japanese word in Japan would elicit such a response. However, she brought clarity to the situation when she informed me that she hadn't heard the word used since pre-World War II. "This is interesting" I thought to myself as images of my plaid spiral notebook sitting patiently on the shelf flashed through my mind. More recently, this same word drew a very similar response from a friend who moved from Japan and has been living in the United States for many years. Definitely another "aha moment" but by this time my plaid spiral notebook was off the bookshelf and accompanying me on my journey.

These experiences of using a word from the Meiji Era which remained a part of Hawai'i Plantation Pidgin but are no longer part of the language spoken in Japan today confirmed for me that isolation can indeed serve as an instrument of preservation.

Of course, as technology advanced and there came a time when a television or two was found in each home, people were introduced to a new influx of the Japanese culture and language. Where regional cultures and languages brought over by the immigrants once thrived, they were now being replaced in favor of what was considered standard Japanese as reflected in and

promoted by the many television broadcasts. The flavor of the dialects was now not only being cast off but looked down upon as well.

The changing flavors, literally, can be seen even in the standardization of foods. A case in point is *ozōni* (*mochi* [rice cake] soup), which is served as part of *osechi* (traditional Japanese New Year's foods). The recipe no longer reflects its homegrown roots of the prefectures but instead is now homogenized to be of a clear soup with *mochi*, carrots, *mizuna* (*Brassica rapa* var. *nipponsinica*) and *shītake* (*Lentinula edodes*). No longer seen are the varied dishes using the specialty items influenced by the geography: Hiroshima seafood and Kumamoto pork and chicken with mountain vegetables including *araimo* (dasheen) and *takenoko* (bamboo shoots).

Even some of the funeral traditions are gone. For instance, unlike today where the menu after the funeral consists of meat, chicken and pork, the food served after the funerals when I was a small child was strictly *shōjin* (vegetarian cuisine). How can I forget those round *musubi* (rice ball), some even sprinkled with black sesame seeds? While these round *musubi* are naturally easier to make than the triangular ones, keep in mind they were only served at funerals. Any child ending up with round *musubi* after failed attempts to make triangular ones was sure to suffer the wrath of the angry mother or grandmother.

Some *obon* (religious observance to honor one's ancestors) traditions are also disappearing. No longer do you see people cleaning and scrubbing the graves as in the past. Floral offerings now replace the *shōjin osonae* (vegetarian offering). The hanging *chōchin* (paper lantern) which adorned the many graves are no longer seen. The *bon odori* (dance following the religious service honoring one's ancestors), however, has gained increasing popularity as a multicultural summer social event. Once involving predominantly Japanese dancers dressed in *yukata* (light cotton *kimono* [traditional Japanese clothing]), it is now enjoyed by community members and visitors alike.

CHAPTER 5

The Influence of WWII on the Japanese in Hawai'i

World War II, I believe, played a significant role in the demise of Hawai'i Plantation Pidgin—The Japanese Way. Those who grew up during this time period reflected on being forbidden to speak any Japanese. This self-imposed non-use resulted from the high possibility of being suspected as a traitor or a spy should one be heard using the language of the enemy. The fact that retaliation came swiftly following the attack on Pearl Harbor sent a strong and definitive message to the Japanese community which remained with them throughout the war. By the evening of December 8, one day after the bombing of Pearl Harbor, 345 Japanese who were considered potentially dangerous to the United States were rounded up by the FBI. Some leaders including Shinto and Buddhist priests, Japanese language school teachers and principals, newspaper editors and community leaders were arrested by local authorities within forty-eight hours of the attack, after the declaration of martial law which continued in Hawai'i until October 24, 1944. These arrests and detentions ensured the vigilance of Japanese in Hawai'i to not be seen as one of the enemy continued. Not only did the Japanese language, but the culture, customs and clothing all disappeared as well.

It seems, however, post-World War II experienced a renaissance of cultural awareness and more recently Hawai'i Plantation Pidgin itself appears to be experiencing a revival particularly in the form of Hawai'i Creole English. A movie buff who loved both *samurai* and Westerns felt this renaissance was due in part to Japanese movies citing a number of movie companies which were in Honolulu during the 1960s such as Daiei Theatre, Kokusai Theatre, Nippon Theatre, Shochiku Theatre, Toho Theater and Toyo Theatre. There were local Japanese radio stations sharing not only the language but popular Japanese music as well. Local Japanese programs were televised live prior to the advent of satellite broadcasting directly from Japan.

One of the things I find particularly interesting is how those who attended elementary school during the war years speak differently as compared to others of the same *sansei* generation including myself. Their speech is more reflective of the English taught in English Standard Schools rather than that of local Pidgin with its particular flavor and accent. This is primarily due to the teachers themselves since many of them were from the Mainland (contiguous United States) and it was only natural the students emulated their manner of speech. Moreover, teachers and principals counseled students to speak English well if they were to be successful in this world. Although many of these students went to the Mainland to earn their teaching degrees, they returned home to become our teachers. Just as we, as *sansei*, were buffered from the influence of our *issei* grandparents by our *nisei* parents, we were buffered by our locally born and raised teachers and not directly influenced by the Mainland teachers. So it was that some of the Japanese pronunciation lost by the impact of the war made its return.

CHAPTER 6

What's in a Name?

I heard an anecdote growing up, which I found amusing at the time, and filed in a drawer somewhere in the back of my mind. Interestingly enough, I heard its storyline once again but this time in the form of an actual experience giving life to the one I heard as a child.

Entitled "Chinese Laundry Man," it goes as follows: "This guy is walking through Chinatown. He is fascinated with all the Chinese restaurants, the Chinese shops, the Chinese signs and banners on the buildings. He is having the best time just walking and looking. He turns a corner and sees a building with a sign, 'Hans Olaffsen's Laundry.' He thinks, 'How in the world does that fit in here?' So he walks into the shop and sees an old Chinese gentleman sitting in the corner. The visitor asks, 'How in the world did this place get a name like Hans Olaffsen's Laundry?' The old man answers, 'Is name of owner.' The visitor asks, 'Well, who in the heck is the owner?' 'I am he' answers the old man. 'You? How in the heck did you ever get a name like Hans Olaffsen?' The old man replies, 'Many years ago when I come to this country, I was standing in line at Documentation Center. Man in front of me was big blonde Swede. Lady look at him and go 'What your name? He say Hans Olaffsen. She look at me… What your name? I say Sam Ting.' (sam ting→ same thing)"

Now for some of the real stories. The Caucasians processing the immigrants asked the Choi family their last name. However, their response of "Ah" before saying their actual last name was mistaken to be part of their name. Hence, this "Ah" and the misspelling of "Choi" resulted in "Ah Choy" which was the official name recorded to become the legacy carried on by their future generations.

There is also the Ah Sam family who received their name because their ancestor's first name was mistaken to be his last name.

Receiving alternate spellings of one's name didn't only occur while going through the documentation line at immigration. My dad's name, for example, was spelled Tameyo on his birth certificate, Tamewo in the 1930 United States Census and subsequently Tameo on his marriage and death certificates.

Creating names was not unique to the government. Children were often judge and jury when coining names and conferring them upon their peers. It seems while growing up during plantation days almost everyone had a nickname, especially if you were a boy. Someone (of the male gender, of course) offered the explanation that the girls would slap the boys if they gave them a nickname resulting in only boys having nicknames. I offer another explanation. Boys, in comparison to girls, tended to play in team sports more often and, therefore, interacted with more people of different ethnic backgrounds. Having nicknames made it easier for other ethnic groups who had difficulty pronouncing Japanese names to identify someone. Nicknames, not to be confused with English names, often provided a bond of closeness and commonality where status or rank were unimportant although the names sometimes were not necessarily of a positive nature.

On the other hand, English names rather than nicknames seemed to be given to girls, particularly as they went on to trade or technical schools or gained employment. Again, this made for easier pronunciation by other ethnic groups. These English names were often times never legalized.

Nicknames were not uncommonly based on a person's physical attributes. For some whose head was perceived to be larger than average, *Big Head* or *Humpty* might have been bestowed upon them. On the other hand, *Pinhead* might be the name given to someone whose head seemed to be smaller than average. Then there were those whose head reminded others of objects because of their shape, such as *Tamago* (egg) and *Torpedo*. Eyes were another feature on which nicknames were based. These names were primarily animal names because their eyes looked like those particular animals— *Cobra*, *Menpachi* (fish belonging to the Holocentridae family) and *Owl* to name a few. The hair, or lack of it, gave names to *Bird Nest* because of a *girigiri* (cowlick), *Cotton* because of his wavy hair and to *Baldhead*. *Baby Deer* was a short guy. *Peanut* was so named because of the build of his body—he was so muscular he looked like a peanut. However, there is another *Peanut* so named because he loved to eat it. It shouldn't be surprising then that *Hunchy* got his name because he walked with a hunched back.

Sometimes how one acted could be the basis of a nickname. As with the eyes, the following names were based on real animals. A skinny guy who wasn't deterred from acting like a *Gorilla* was given this name. A small guy got the name *Spider* because he crawled like a spider. How *Cock-a-Roach* aka *Kakaruch* (derivatives of cockroach) received his name, I cannot even begin to guess.

Nicknames could sometimes be tricky, too. *Monk* sounds like he would be a religious person but his friends say he got his name because he looked like a monkey. And while it would tend to reason having *Football* as a nickname meant he was a good football player, in this case it was because his head was shaped like a football. *Okino* is a Japanese name but it has nothing to do with this man's name. One version is that he was like a *sumō* (sport of wrestling in Japan) wrestler. Another version is that he actually received this name as a description of a particular physical attribute. One day while he was using the bathroom, a friend standing in the next stall happened to look down at him and commented, "*ōkī no...*" (*ōkī* is big in Japanese, *no*, a discourse particle).

Comic strips, movies and even nursery rhymes were sources for nicknames. For instance, the cartoon character *Sluggo* from the *Sluggo and Nancy* comic strip seemed to be a fairly popular nickname for those whose heads resembled his bald one. *Fantaz* was named from the comic strip Fantasma. *Gijo* was given this name when he mistakenly identified a G.I. Joe movie. Although he read Joe as it should be, he read G.I. as *gi*. *Tiger* got his name from a movie although no one could recall which one. The nursery rhyme, "Georgie Porgie pudding and pie" served as the basis for the nickname *Po'gie*.

Where one lived or lived by could become the nickname with which you were associated. So it happened with *Anpan* (bread roll filled with bean paste) who lived next to the bakery.

Clothing was another aspect that identified someone. *Timoshenko* got his name because he wore a Russian jacket which made him look like a Russian general. *German* got his name because during World War II he rode around on a bicycle wearing a German hat.

Even a vehicle, or its part, could be someone's claim to fame as well. While *Gangster* (*Gangsta'*) drove the family car which looked similar to that of the notorious Al Capone, *Karinkarin* might have gotten his name from the possible perceived onomatopoetic sound of the bicycle bell.

There are names whose origins remain a mystery. How did all three brothers come to be known as *Cowboy* when none of them knew how to ride a horse? Were they wild? How did *Garoot* (go-fer) get his name? Some say it's because he was rascal. Is *Pandoro* known for stealing bread from the bakery next door or dropping it and making it dirty as he was carrying it across the street? (*pan* is the Japanese word for bread which is of Portuguese origin; *dorobo* is thief; *doro* is mud) And what did *Mikandoro* do to get his name? (*Mikan* is orange in Japanese) And what about *Mamankibi* (corn)?" Did he like corn, was he a corny guy, or did he have some physical feature similar to corn?

Nicknames are really another reflection of the spirit of the Hawai'i Plantation Pidgin culture. Even those of Japanese ethnicity were given nicknames of different languages. The oldest brother of ten boys in one family came to be called *Papale* (hat) *hemo* (take off) because he was the only one circumcised. *Pipi* (beef) worked with calves at a ranch. Then there was another Japanese who was given a Chinese name, *Sansan*, although his last name didn't correlate with this Chinese reading. (In Chinese, *san tian* denotes a Japanese surname or place name such as Mita, Sanda, or Mitsuda as reflected in the characters 三田.)

Nicknames were also famously or infamously given for what one was recognized. This was the case for *Dengi* who was the first dengue fever patient on Hawai'i Island. He contracted this infectious tropical disease while picking pineapple in Honolulu and returned home with it. *Gaji* was famous, or infamous, for hiding his *gaji* (wild) card when playing *hanafuda* (Japanese playing cards). There were a couple of fishing buddies who were known as *Dr. Papio* (young stage of a giant trevally, a fish) and *Mr. Uhu* (parrot fish). *Taggy*, not surprisingly, was known to be a tag along. *Fishbone* got his name because would bring fish bones for lunch when it was time to cut the cane. My uncle was *Broken* because he loved to eat "crack (broken) seed." The nickname *General Tire* was given in recognition of this baseball player's skill. Every time someone hit a home run they were awarded with a tire. While *Nuts*, his friends say, was the crazy guy.

There were also names which gave recognition for what one was known to do but tended to be of more dubious distinction like *Buss up* who was always looking for a fight and *Chuggalator* who consumed great amounts of alcohol.

Then there were nicknames which for reasons often unknown took on a different pronunciation as in the case of brothers *Big Dopey* and *Small Dopey* who came to be known as *Dobey*.

Sometimes nicknames were contraction of nicknames. Perhaps it may have been to distinguish people apart. Such may have been the case of the *Kabakaba* (*kaba* is defined as hippopotamus; birch; cattail) brothers where the older one was eventually called *Kaba* while the younger one remained *Kabakaba*.

Nicknames were also somehow derived from the actual name itself. As with many words of Hawai'i Plantation Pidgin which were often contracted, names were also shortened using no more than the first and second syllables or even only initials. This might be the result of the length of Japanese names which could be three or four syllables. *Masa* might be the nickname for various names such as "Masanobu," "Masayuki" or "Masaaki." There's *Taz* for "Tazuko" and *Sue* for "Sueko." It is interesting to note here that the change in spelling sometimes changed the pronunciation to a more anglicized version as in *Taz* which was pronounced like the "Tas" in "Tasmania" rather than the "Ta" in "Tacoma." Sue was pronounced "sou" as in "soup" although it is actually two syllables and should have been pronounced "sou" as in "soup" and "a" as in the first letter of the alphabet. My uncles and my mother were known by their initials—*N* for Nobuo, *Y* for Yasushi and *T* for Tsurue. Chiyoko was known as *C*. This "initializing factor," so to speak, is still reflected today where Jane is called *J* and Vivian goes by *V*.

A nickname derived from the actual name can even be bilingual. Such is the case for *Sugar* whose English nickname is based on an abbreviation of his Japanese name, Satoshi. *Satō* is the Japanese word for sugar although the character for Satoshi and the character for sugar are different.

Saying a name backwards was another way in which nicknames were created. Sadao became "*O(a)das*, Takeshi became *Shiket* and Fred became *Derf*.

Family lines showed up in nicknames as well. There's *Puppy* and his younger brother, *Small Puppy*, *Bing Crosby* and his younger brother, *Small Bing Crosby*, and *Dango* (dumpling) and his younger brother, *Small Dango*.

Other names identified what they or their parents either sold or peddled such as *Fish* and *Moyashi* (bean sprouts).

Nicknames were not given to individuals alone. For instance, the baseball teams in Kea'au had them. The village team was known as *Townies*, the Filipino team was called *Filanks*, the team at 8-Mile Camp was named *Aces*, and the team at 9-Mile Camp was referred to as "*Blues*" and hence 9-Mile Camp was also known as "Blues Camp."

No matter the manner in how a nickname came about, they were a just part of growing up in the "good old days" of plantation life.

CHAPTER 7

Hanabata Days

Walking down memory lane would just not be complete without remembering those days when the stain of nasal mucus dirtied your face as it ran down. Wiping it was never a priority because it was never distracting. Or if you did wipe it, you didn't bother looking for tissue because, after all, the sleeves of whatever you were wearing at the time served the purpose. These were the good old days of childhood, often referred to as the "*hanabata* (liquid nasal mucus) days." Derived from the Japanese word for nose, *hana*, and the English, *butter*, this particular butter found its way into the mouths of an untold number of children a countless number of times.

Hanabata tends to be more liquid in nature and is often soft and gooey as compared to its counterpart, *hanakuso* (dried nasal mucus) which is hard and dry. The use of the term *–kuso* (excrement) is often heard as it refers to waste from different body parts such as *mekuso* (eye discharge or mucus) and *mimikuso* (earwax), terms common to both Hawai'i and Japan. *Hesokuso* (belly button lint) is used in Hawai'i rather than in Japan where *heso no goma* is heard. However, the top honors in usage frequency of this *-kuso* family goes to *hanakuso* although it still remains in second place when compared to *hanabata*.

Let us now capture the spirit of childhood as we visit during playtime on the plantation. While the days of youth sometimes involved a lot of hard work—helping in the cane fields, tending to the backyard vegetable garden and taking care of younger siblings among other responsibilities—there were times when caution could be thrown to the wind and the neighborhood children would gather to share the carefree joys known only in childhood. It is important to include this section because it was during these carefree times when we played with friends that we learned not only about the importance of values, cultures and fair play but we also learned to communicate.

As we address the role games played and the ingenuity that gave birth to some of them, it is important to keep in mind that the plantation way of life was austere and frugal. "No mo' money" ("No more money"→"There is no money") was a way of life. Whatever was earned through the hard work of daily toil was needed for life's necessities. There was no extra to buy children's games or toys. But, as with children anywhere, it was only natural that the social lives of the plantation children included games. In our world today, games and toys can be easily purchased at the store or by going online. This was not the case in plantation days when the children had to use their resourcefulness and imagination to create and improvise games and toys from what was free and available.

Flowers and their buds quickly transformed in children's clever hands. From its bright orange flowers and flower buds full of water, the African tulip (*Spathodea campanulata*) quickly became nature's water gun for the children's picking. I'm not sure if it's because the buds shot out water as if in the act of urinating or because their liquid had a not too pleasant odor but this tree was sometimes referred to as the *shishi* (urine, urination; to

urinate) tree. I've heard it called "piss tree" as well but I am sure this is a term of more current times. There was also the hibiscus whose sticky stamen became a perfect adornment for sticking onto the nose. Its sweet nectar, too, was a source of delight for the palate.

Fruits were another wonderful gift from nature. A papaya took on the role of a jack-o-lantern because it would have been too wasteful to buy a pumpkin simply for this purpose. Bubbles were unavailable for purchase at the store so instead detergent was placed in the papaya stem and blown. The *jabon* (pomelo) provided safety gear for football. By slicing the skin into wedges, two of them were used as shoulder pads with the remaining skin serving as the helmet.

Even grasses proved to be a wonderful resource. A game was played using the *popolo* aka *polopolo* grass or black nightshade (*Solanum nigrum*) whereby the fruit of the grass was placed on top of the grass like an umbrella and blowing it with California grass split open. The object was to see how long it could be kept up in the air. Additionally, the plant was valued medicinally and its edible small black berries were available as a snack. Its young shoots and leaves were also eaten as greens. The *hōsenko* or garden balsam (*Impatiens balsamina*) made wonderful earrings because its green pods could be snapped onto the ears.

Stilts were made from cans. Tuna cans were used for lower ones while cream and other taller cans provided for higher ones. Stilts were also called "horse" because they made a loud "clop, clop, clop" sound, much like a horse, when someone walked with them.

Innovation and fun often overruled safety factors. A game called "buzz saw" was created by flattening a metal cap from a soda bottle, putting a hole in the middle and threading a string through it. By holding both ends of the string and twirling it until the string tightened, a buzz saw like sound was emitted when pulled on both sides. The sound continued as the string was repeatedly released and tightened. Sometimes the top of a can, such as a tuna can, was used. Of course, a safer version was using paper milk caps.

Then there was the slingshot. It was often made with the Y part of the guava branch or depending on how you looked at it, the V. This part was also referred to as the *mata* (fork in the branch). The tube of a tire was used for the rubber strips, the leather taken from boots or the tongue of the shoe served as the pocket, and *pilau maile* (*Parderia scandens* formerly *Parderia foetida*) or *honohono* (*Commelina diffusa*) grass was used for the projectile.

Perhaps it would not considered a game but a common past time for children was to mimic their parents and other adults smoking since the Surgeon General's report warning about the negative effects of cigarette smoking didn't appear until January 11, 1964. Rolling Bull Durham was not something out of the ordinary. While I never smoked it, I remember rolling it for my *obāchan* until she passed away when I was five. Children created their own version of cigarettes from non-tobacco products such as California grass, dried anthurium stems, dried guava leaves and rolled banana leaves.

While the above games provided hours of enjoyment and camaraderie, I would like to now address some games which have contributed to terminology of Hawai'i Plantation Pidgin. The terminology may have resulted possibly from geographical differences with each locale, or camp, having its own dialect. Or they may have resulted from a "mis" or two, that is, misunderstanding or mishearing of the source, misremembering, mispronunciation and misspelling. All these factors, I believe, were important in creating words which are part of Hawai'i Plantation Pidgin.

Bean Bags *(Ojami)*

Playing *ojami* was, to me, much like playing the Japanese version of jacks. It consisted of three bean bags often filled with either Job's Tears or Black-eyed Susie's. Rice was also sometimes used although I imagine its use as a food source outranked its use as a stuffing for toys. The object was to be the first in completing the increasingly difficult levels of play. If a player did not successfully complete a level, it was the next player's turn.

While the game is certainly reminiscent of childhood, it is discussed here because its metamorphosis in spelling and pronunciation, seemingly influenced by the American spelling, then led to a different pronunciation. The "*mi*" in "*ojami*" is pronounced like the American spelling of "me." Therefore, when written in English, "*ojami*" became "*ojame*" which then changed its pronunciation from "me" to a pronunciation closer to "may" when read from the Japanese Romanization standpoint.

Chōchi chōchi

An interactive game played with babies, *Chōchi chōchi* is still played today. The Hawai'i version is somewhat different in its words and motions compared with the Japanese version but they both still provide wonderful opportunities for bonding!

Chōchi chōchi	Clap hands twice (on each *chōchi*)
A wa wa	Place open hand on open mouth on each syllable
Kaikuri kaikuri	With elbows bent and arms in front, place right arm above left arm and move in a circular motion, first right arm moving forward away from your body simultaneously with the left arm moving backward toward your body on the first *kaikuri*, then alternate motion on the second *kaikuri* with the right arm moving toward your body and the left arm moving away from your body
Atama tenten	Tap head with fist on each *ten*
Ohara ponpon	Tap stomach with open hand on each *pon*
Jōzu jōzu	Clap several times—this is the "yay, you did it" part

This game is included here because there is thought that the words *Chōchi chōchi* may be derived from "Church church" and the clapping of the hands symbolizes hands in prayer.

Kamapio, A Game of Many Names

There was a game played on the plantation which would be considered dangerous by today's standards but was commonplace then. Someone I spoke with actually got his eye poked when he was four while crossing the yard to get home. Similar to baseball, the object was to get the batter out.

This game was played throughout Hawai'i Island but depending upon the geographical location was known by different names. The first time I heard about the game from Kea'au and Hilo people, they called it *kamapio.* A friend in Hakalau knew it as *alapio.* Yet another friend who grew up in Pāhoa knew it as *kanapio.* Then a Pa'auilo person informed me he did some research on Pidgin and heard it as *kanapio* in Pa'auilo and then not again until Pāhala. A Hilo person wrote it in her story as *okamapio.* The Japanese add "o" to words to make them honorific such as *kāsan* to *okāsan* for mother and *bentō* to *obentō* for Japanese box lunch. I do not know whether this "o" was added as an afterthought to make it an honorific term or whether it has nothing to do with being an honorific word. Finally, after thinking I had heard all the names of this game, another friend said she knew it as *kamepio* in Kalapana where she played it with her mom during summer fun.

I was intrigued that there were so many names for this one game and to make sure everyone was talking about the same game I asked them to describe it. There seems to be some variations but basically from what I can surmise, it is definitely the same game. The items for the game itself were two sticks, either a broomstick or a branch approximately twenty inches which was used as the bat, a shorter stick approximately six inches sharpened at both ends which was used as the ball (it was this that was called the *pio*) and two similar-sized rocks on which to place the broomstick across to form a bridge. Burlap bags were commonly used as the gloves to catch the *pio* otherwise bare hands were skillfully used.

It is still amazing that this game, now years after it is no longer played and has become but a memory filed somewhere in the back of people's minds long after they've reached adulthood, can still be identified to the locale where it was played by what it is called. A friend mentioned to me that her friend told her about a game called *alapio*. Being from Pāhoa, she knew the game only as *kanapio*. When I asked her if her friend was from Hakalau, she replied in the affirmative and queried me as to how I knew. My explanation elicited a "That's so cool, you have to share it" response and so it is here being shared. A successor to this game, with variations, is called "crack bat."

Marbles aka Agates

The object of the game was to acquire your opponents' marbles. Different names were indicative of the different styles of marbles. One person's understanding, however, could be different from another. For example, one person's recollection is *talanka* refers to the titanium marble; *bambucha* refers to the glass cat's eye marble; and yet another marble is referred to as *barbarians*. Another person's interpretation is *talanka* is really the glass marble and those titanium marbles are not actually marbles but ball bearings. When I heard this explanation, I thought it made sense. After all, to a child whose hearing may not be so discriminating and whose vocabulary may not contain "ball bearings," *barbarians* might just be the perfect name for that "metallic marble."

The names used for the big marble or shooter are certainly worth a mention here—*talank, talanka, talanko, talompa, bambaluta, bambucha, bambuchi, bambula* and *bandola*. The variations in these names may be due either to geographical differences or ethnic origins. The closeness in pronunciations could also be the outcome of either the misunderstanding or mishearing of the source due perhaps to an unfamiliar accent or vocabulary resulting in new words or variations of a word—a prime example of creating new words as they are heard.

CHAPTER 8

Jan Ken Po

The discussion of games would be incomplete without *Jan Ken Po*, a game played to pass time or more often as a decision-making tool to determine an outcome. Among other decisions, it was played to see who would go first in other games such as "Marbles," to determine who got to be line leader, who got dibs on an item or who had to wipe the table after dinner. Its rhythmic mantra was heard everywhere. For the reason its language evolution is an exemplary reflection of the evolution of Hawai'i Plantation Pidgin itself, it is included here as its own chapter and not as part of games.

This hand game usually played by two people requires no equipment, only their outstretched hands. On the designated cue word, usually understood to be the last word or syllable in the recitation, each participant shows in an almost throwing manner the forms of rock, paper or scissors. Rock, represented by a closed fist, beats scissors because it can damage the scissors by hitting it; paper, represented by an open hand, beats rock because it can cover the rock; and scissors, represented by the outstretched index and middle fingers symbolizing the blades of a scissors, beats paper because it can cut it. Should the same item be shown by both participants, the game is considered a tie and is replayed until a winner is determined. This was often two out of three games.

There seems to be various versions recited in Japan, but I have chosen the following which I learned from two sisters to be the standard:

1st line:	*Saisho wa gū*	First is rock
2nd line:	*Jan ken poi (pon)*	
3rd line:	*Ai ko desho*	No winner yet.

I never heard of the 1st line and no one among those I spoke to in Hawai'i ever mentioned it. Somehow it seems not to have made it over from Japan and for that reason it is not being included here. In the 2nd line, the *pon* is in parentheses because although it is not what the sisters in Japan recite, I have heard it and seen it written this way in both Japan and Hawai'i.

The following two lines recited in the past seem to have altogether disappeared from the recitation in Hawai'i although they are still heard in some dialects of Japan.

| 4th line: | *Mada mada ikenai* | Still not yet |
| 5th line: | *Mō ichido* | One more time |

In Hawai'i, the first line is recited either as:

| 1st line: | *Jan ken po* or |
| 1st line: | *Jan kena po* |

While the first syllable *jan* remains intact, the third syllable has changed from its original Japanese version. The *n* at the end of *pon* is no longer recited leaving only the *po*. The second syllable *ken* has been retained in one version, but *na* has replaced the *n* in another version. It is the third syllable, however, I find unusual in that the *n* has been totally dropped at the very end. This tends to be contrary to other Hawai'i Plantation Pidgin words in which *n* is the sound usually retained, not the one being eliminated when contracting standard Japanese into local speech. An example is *iran* contracted from *irimasen* meaning "not needed." The *ri* is replaced by *ra* and *n* is retained. Another example is *akan* from *akemasen* meaning "cannot open" where the *ke* is replaced by *ka* and *n* is retained.

The changes in the second line are where I thought things got really interesting. It was so interesting I logged these changes in what I deduced could be their possible evolution as seen here.

2nd line: *Ai ko desho*

Ai kono sho

~~*Ai kano sho/Ai kona sho*~~

Ai kana sho

Ai kena sho

I canna' show.

I cannot show.

I'm gonna show.

I no can show.

The standard Japanese version of *Ai ko desho* may still be heard but seems to be rarely used. In what seems to be the first change, the *de* was dropped and replaced with *no* resulting in *Ai kono sho*. In the second change, *Ai kana sho*, the *kono* has been replaced by *kana*. You'll see in my list I have a change of *kano* and another of *kona* between these two changes. It is there because to my ears it seems either could have been the next step in the sound progression. In other words, I thought the change of one syllable at a time *kono* to *kano* or *kona* seemed to be a logical progression rather than changing both o's (*kono*) to both a's (*kana*) at the same time. However, because I did not hear it among those with whom I spoke, they are crossed off and at this point remain simply as placeholders. The third change to A*i kena sho* is where I thought it went from really interesting to really, really interesting…at least, I think it does. Here, the *ka* has changed to *ke* going from *kana* to *kena*. I feel this is significant in that it is the pivotal point where it transitions from being basically Japanese to becoming English. It is this and the following line which, to me, serves as the epitome of the evolution of *Jan Ken Po* and is an exemplary reflection of the evolution of Hawai'i Plantation Pidgin itself. When you compare the sound of *Ai kena sho* to the next change of "I canna' show," the difference is distinct although slight. Said quickly, however, the difference is almost imperceptible. Another interesting, if not significant, point is the syllable *sho*. While it is in the form of a Japanese syllable in *Ai kena sho* of the Japanese version, it becomes an English word—that is to say, the word "show" in the English version of "I canna' show." I cannot determine whether they are equivalent to each other or have nothing to do with each other but I cannot help but think it makes for interesting contemplation.

The "canna'" in "I canna' show" is a typical example of the contraction style seen frequently in Hawai'i Plantation Pidgin. So it is logical that if one uses the standard English word from which it is derived that "I cannot show" logically follows. In the following two lines, the local speech again comes into play. The "gonna" in "I'm gonna show" is again reflective of the contraction style and is derived from the standard English "going to" while "I no can show" is, in my opinion, Pidgin English.

The ending third line of yesteryear's version which did not seem to not have been recited by all players is *Jan kena man kena sakasakapo*. Similar with other words which were contracted or dropped, I thought this line may have met that fate. But I should've known better knowing that language is alive and always evolving. My nine-year old *hānai* (foster) grandson updated me on a version which is recited as *Junk and a monk and a sakasakapo*. Other spellings of this version include *Junk an' a monk an' a socka socka po* and *Junk and a munk and sokka sokka po*. These variations remind us that different spellings will occur since Hawai'i Plantation Pdigin's purpose was to serve as verbal rather than as written communication. I soon learned this is not the only recitation as the evolution continues.

One person with whom I spoke was about to prophesize what I would soon hear. She said, "I never used to say the *shakashakapo* part, but nowadays people say that." So it happened one morning I was awakened to my five-year old *hānai* grandson running down the hall chanting, *Junk and a monk and a shakashakapo*. Not only did he and his brother quickly affirm that the line is indeed still alive and well but as with the rest of *Jan Ken Po*, it too, had been transformed. And this time it was, I am guessing, *shakashaka* may have been an influence from the Hawaiian hand sign, "shaka," for "hi," "thank you," "hang loose" and other things conveying the Aloha Spirit and expressing the friendship, understanding and compassion among the cultures in Hawai'i.

It seems the children on the plantations did not have a monopoly on creativity as the children of today seem to have invented yet another version which my seven year-old *hānai* granddaughter shared with me. It is recited as follows:

> "Tic tac toe.
> Give me an X,
> Give me an O—
> Give me three in a row.
> Tic tac toe.

Tic tac toe.

Tic tac toe."

The last three "Tic tac toe" lines are played like *Jan Ken Po* where paper, rock or scissors is shown. Should one player win all three games, that player goes on to say either, "I win, you lose, now you get a big bruise" or "I win, you lose, now you get a small bruise." The big bruise consists of a fist. The loser is hit on the arm with the flat end of the winner's fist (the side where the baby finger is located). The small bruise is administered with two fingers, the thumb and the index finger, and the loser is touched lightly as if being pinched.

The *Jan Ken Po* game seems to have its origin in China dating back to sometime during the Han Dynasty, 206 B.C–220 A.D. After its import to Japan as a Chinese drinking game sometime in the 17th century, history shows these *ken* (hand games) were also popular as foreplay in the brothels. By the early 20th century, this game had spread beyond Asia, particularly because of Japan's increased contact with the west and seems to have become popular in Europe by the late 1920s. In Britain, it was described in a letter to a newspaper as a hand game in 1924, followed by the appearances of a thriller entitled "Scissors Cut Paper" in 1927 and "Stone Blunts Scissors" in 1929. In France, it was described in detail in a children's magazine in 1927, and was called *chi-fou-mi* based on the Japanese words *hi, fu, mi* for "one, two, three." The rules of this game were also described in a New York Times article in 1932.

The game is called *jak-en-poy* in the Philippines, a possible transliteration from the Japanese *jan ken poi*. The Japanese influence here is not surprising since Japan occupied the Philippines from 1942 to 1945 during World War II.

Malaysia and Singapore have a different version in which "scissors" is replaced by "bird." Additionally, Singapore has a related hand game of *ji gu pa* which may also be a transliteration of the names of the hand gestures of the original Japanese *jan ken po* game, that is, *choki* (scissors), *gū* (rock) and *pā* (paper).

Jan Ken Po, it appears, is a game which has transcended time and cultures not only in Hawaiʻi but internationally as well. Numerous variations of this game have been created across many personal and societal fronts from the simple changes in objects to video games, weapons and more rules. It has been used in resolving litigation and million dollar issues. However, for the children on the plantations, it was just a game reflective of the carefree times of a simpler life.

CHAPTER 9

Plantation Terms

There were terms created specifically for the sugar cane plantations which described some aspect of work or life and were often derived from combining words from the different languages used on the plantations. Other terms were adopted from these languages but came to have their own distinct meaning almost to the exclusion of other definitions. Although the definition remain unchanged in its language of origin, its interpreted and applied use on the plantations were so dominant that it was not seen as being from a particular language or having its own definition in that language. As is characteristic of Hawai'i Plantation Pidgin, the originating languages of these words and phrases were unimportant.

The words shared here are but a modest representation of both created and adopted terms of the plantation.

Bangō

Bangō, adopted from the Japanese word for "number," referred to the system and to the numbers themselves which identified workers on the plantations. It functioned much like the numbers of the Social Security program which began in 1935. The *bangō* system dictated financial transactions of the laborers on the plantation by providing a more accurate means for the

accounting of payroll including overtime pay, store purchases, laundry services, deductions for infractions and other money-related activities. Plantation owners claimed this system was easier because it avoided misspellings and mispronunciation of foreign names and saved time, a commodity highly valued in the plantations.

Upon arrival each worker was assigned a number and given a *bangō* tag. The plantations usually made these silver dollar-sized tags out of brass or aluminum with the worker's assigned number printed on one side. Numbers were assigned by ethnic groups as follows:

1 – 899	Japanese aliens
900 – 1400	Japanese-Americans or Hawaii-born Japanese
2000 – 2100	Portuguese
2200	Spanish
2300	Hawaiian
2400	Puerto Rican
3000	Chinese or Korean
4000 & 5000	Filipino aliens
5900 & above	Filipino–Americans

Hapai hara and Hapai ko

Hapai, the contracted Pidgin version of the Hawaiian word *hāpai* meaning "to carry; bear, lift; elevate; raise; hoist; hold up" was sometimes used in combination with words of other languages to describe certain tasks in the fields. For instance, combined with the Japanese pronunciation of the English word "harrow," *hapai hara* meant "carry the harrow or plow." Combined with the contracted Pidgin version of the Hawaiian word *kō* for sugar cane, *hapai ko* literally meant "to carry sugar cane." This job was not as simplistic as it may sound. It involved cutting the cane stalks close to the ground, bundling the stalks so that they could be lifted onto the workers' shoulders, and then carrying these bundles from the fields where they were cut to ox carts so that they could be transported to the mills. Done throughout the six-day work week for ten hours a day under the watchful eye of the *luna, hapai ko* was physically demanding and grueling work.

Hippari men

Hippari men was coined from the Japanese word *hipparu*, "to pull," and the English word "men." It referred to the younger, stronger workers who were paid more to set artificially faster paces for their fellow workers. Their collaboration with plantation management earned them much hatred from their fellow workers who often threw sticks and stones at them to slow them down. There is even a documented case that occurred in December 1893 in which a *hippari man* was bound and beaten for not keeping his word to not set a fast pace.

Hoe hana

Hoe hana was the term resulting from the English word "hoe" and the Hawaiian word *hana* meaning "work or labor." It originally meant doing hoe work in the cane fields, that is, weeding the cane rows by hoe. This term, however, did not only describe the act of doing the hoe work itself but embodied the concept of "working together." Each person's cooperation was essential in order to accomplish the task efficiently and effectively. Everyone needed to stand in a straight line and everyone needed to take a step together in order for the line to move together. *Hoe hana* is now used as a general term of doing work with a hoe such as digging or weeding in the yard or garden.

Holehole bushi

Holehole bushi was derived from the Hawaiian word *holehoele*, "to strip dried sugar cane leaves from the stalk," and the Japanese word *bushi*, "song or melody." Also known as Japanese plantation songs, these songs composed by the immigrant Japanese workers reflected the hardship, suffering and uncertainty of their life in Hawai'i. Since the *holehole* work was considered less demanding than other work and was typically a woman's job, it is believed that women probably composed most of the earlier songs.

Kachi ken

The Japanese pronunciation of the English "cut cane," *kachi ken* is an example of the non-importance of a word's originating language. It was adopted and spoken as part of the Japanese used on the plantation. Other words typical of this are *bosh men*, the Japanese pronunciation of the English "boss man" for "boss;" and *big(g)u shotto*, the Japanese pronunciation of the English "big shot" to describe an important person.

Kompa(n[g])

The word *kompa* seems to have evolved from the Filipino pronunciation of *companion* to *kompanion* with *kompa kompa* and *kompa(n[g])* as the resulting terms commonly used. Originally meaning "sugar cane cultivation by a small group who shared work together," *kompa* has come to embrace the spirit of sharing as a way of life on the plantation, both at work and in the community. At work on the plantations, lunch time was often considered the best time because everyone shared their *bento*. Because some went hunting and some went fishing there was something different to share almost daily. Even when the plantations ceased operations, neighbors continued sharing vegetables grown in their gardens or items they cooked or baked. Today, you will find people still share food and vegetables with their friends and neighbors.

Kompa, apparently, is also a foreign-loan word now used in Japan when referring to a type of drinking gathering of university students at an *izakaya* (a casual drinking establishment). This student version tends to be more relaxed than the traditional more formal *nomikai* (a drinking gathering phenomenon particular to the Japanese culture). Although the exact root of this particular *kompa* is unknown, suggestions are that it may have originally come from the German *kompanie,* the English *company* or the French *compagnie.*

Ukupau, Ukepau, Uekibi

These innovative pay systems were developed as incentives for the laborers. As compared to that of the day labor system these systems allowed the laborers to leave when the work was completed rather than working a set number of hours. *Ukupau* is a Hawaiian word defined as "piece labor, pay by the job rather than according to time, as on sugar plantations" and "contract labor." *Ukepau,* derived from the Japanese word *uke,* "to contract; to undertake," and the Hawaiian word *pau,* for "finished or completed," provided for agreed upon work quotas for the day. Then there is *uekibi* which in 1895 further refined the *ukepau* system. I believe the term *uekibi* may be derived from the Japanese words *ue(ru),* "to plant or to grow" and *satōkibi* for "sugar." This system contracted a group of laborers to cultivate a section of cane which organized itself, without a *luna,* managing the work process on its own. I have also heard in my discussions *okupau* and *hukipau* which could be due to geographical differences or mishearings of *ukupau* and *ukepau.*

Sugar

"…that which we call a rose by any other name would smell as sweet" says Juliet to Romeo in the William Shakespeare play, *Romeo and Juliet.* If I may adapt this to "A word by any other name might its meaning remain the same?"

It seems the evolution of Hawai'i Plantation Pidgin as reflected in the game *Jan Ken Po* has a counterpart among the terms used in the sugar cane plantations. I present here the word "sugar" for your consideration. The changes in "sugar" may be attributed to the time period during which it was used. *Satō* (the Japanese word for "sugar") was heard in an earlier time of plantation days while *shuga* (the Japanese pronunciation of the English word "sugar") came about during a later period. The word *satō* was brought by the immigrants and would have been spoken as a natural part of their vocabulary. As interaction with other ethnic groups increased and the necessity for effective communication became essential, foreign words such as *sugar* were introduced. These words then naturally became a part of their vocabulary but would have been pronounced with the Japanese accent whereupon *sugar* became *shuga*. In this case, *sugar* probably referred to the refined sugar or the end product of the cane production process rather than to the sugar cane itself.

The word *satōkibi* which does include *satō* as a part of it is the actual term for "sugar cane." *Kō*, a Hawaiian word also refers to the *sugar cane* rather than to the refined sugar but like many words of Hawai'i Plantation Pidgin has been contracted and is often heard as *ko*. As in the case of "sugar" becoming *shuga*, "cane" became *ken* and "sugar cane" was then called *shuga ken*. Because the Japanese word *ken* means "prefecture," *ken* became a pun among the Hawai'i Japanese when asked from which *ken* one was from. The answer was "*Shuga ken*." While the answer indicated that one was born in Hawai'i, I cannot help but feel that there was a sharing of kindred spirit in it as well.

Cocksucker

There are words, too, which seemingly have multiple definitions but rather their definitions may just be a difference in perception.

"Cocksucker" was seen as a brown noser or a tattletaler. I am guessing that if someone tattletales that they are probably trying to get on someone's good side and is kissing up to them, hence, brown nosing. Perhaps this is how the *luna* got to be referred to as "cocksuckers" since they snitched on the workers so they could look good in management's eyes. Even their hat was referred to as a "cocksucker's hat."

Liliko

Liliko, lili from *li'ili'i*, for bits or to scatter and *ko* from *kō* (sugar cane), for example, took on different perspectives by different people. One viewpoint was that it was the pieces of cane left after hand-cutting or mechanical harvesting occurred. In other words, whatever was left after the major portion of the cane was pushed was called *liliko*. Another viewpoint was that *liliko* referred to the people who picked up the cane along the road after it fell from the truck. On Maui, it referred to small cane and was called *kolili* rather than *liliko* as it was on Hawai'i Island.

Pakiki

The word *pakiki* from *pa'akikī* by definition is "hard, tough, unyielding; arbitrary, inflexible, compact, difficult, stubborn, obstinate." It has come to describe human traits as well as that of inanimate objects such as a nail. It has also been used to describe the human characteristic of being tight. As someone said this word may be an example of being used because of its commonality and familiarity although more appropriate words could be used.

[CHAPTER 10]

Food for Thought

Food is always on my mind. It is, after all, the sustenance of life. I must admit, however, that I do not necessarily eat to live but rather live to eat. I have even been accused of promoting food porn in my photography as it is one of my major themes alongside that of nature and art.

Although it may be the same today, during the days of the sugar plantation communities, food was just as much a subsistence issue as it was a sustenance issue. Food eventually took on a special role becoming its own culture serving to bring people together. This was probably a foreseeable course since by virtue of different ethnic foods representing their respective cultures, eating them naturally brought people closer to that culture. As people interacted more with each other, their communication about different topics and themes, including food, increased as well. Talking about various foods naturally led to the introduction of words whose origins are truly food for thought. Here are a selected few about which I have contemplated and still continue contemplating.

The word *bōbura* (pumpkin) I believed came to Hawai'i via Japan probably from the Kumamoto immigrants. *Abóbora*, the Portuguese word for "pumpkin" was introduced to Japan by Portuguese sailors around 1541 and is derived from *Cambodia abóbora* meaning "Cambodian pumpkin." While Eastern Japan retained *kabocha* (from Cambodia) to mean "pumpkin," Kyushu seems to have accepted *bōbura*. This brings me to the question of how is it that *bōbura* came to be used by the Japanese in Hawai'i. Was it because it was brought over by the Japanese immigrants? Or was it because it was already in use by the Portuguese whose arrival preceded that of the Japanese and, therefore, heard and then adopted by the Japanese who immigrated to Hawai'i? Or is it that both situations coexisted and served only to strengthen the word's existence in Hawai'i?

Then there is the word *bobo* which probably shares no real connection to *abóbora* other than sharing the letters "b, o, b, o" in that particular order. A Portuguese word meaning "fool; silly; idiot; imbecile; stupid," it was commonly used while I growing up. *Bobo* was often used in conjunction with "head" and hearing *bobo head* was not at all uncommon.

The origin of *kaukau* is often discussed now as it was when I was growing up. Some thought it was of Chinese origin while others considered it to be of Hawaiian origin. Some of the Chinese and the Hawaiians with whom I spoke were also uncertain while others were of very definite opinions. For the longest time I believed it to be of Chinese origin coming from the reduplication of the word *chow* for "food." *Chow* apparently derives from Chinese Pidgin English and its introduction into American English in 1856 as "food" had its origins in California. The reduplication is of the Chinese word *cha* or *tsa* meaning "mixed." However, during my research to write this book, I am inclined to think it is from the Hawaiian word *pākaukau* for "table, counter, stand, booth, desk; formerly a long mat on which food was placed (*kaukau*)."

A word which I assumed to be of Japanese origin and did not even consider it to be of another origin was *saimin*. I remember as

a child seeing it often spelled as *saimein* on many menus. Others recalled this spelling as well. It did not occur to me that this spelling might have been a clue to the word's Chinese origin. Apparently, *sai* is the Chinese word for "thin" and *mein* the Chinese word for "Chinese wheat flour noodles." Or could it be that *sai* may be derived from the Japanese word for "vegetables," *yasai*? *Saimin* is a dish whose very existence is an exemplary model reflecting the assimilation of cultures from which it may have come. Not only may it be the result of the Chinese and Japanese cultures but it may have roots in other cultures as well such as the Filipino dish, *pancit*. It also shares similarities with Okinawa *soba* (Japanese buckwheat noodles) in its noodle and broth. The toppings certainly can consist of an array of foods typical of many cultures. It is speculated that perhaps green onions came from the Filipinos, eggs from the

Hawaiians, sausage from the Portuguese and cabbage from the Koreans. Additionally, the topping often includes an item frequently identified with Hawaii's cuisine—spam.

The final word I would like to discuss here is *mamansan* (*manmansan*). As with *kaukau*, its origins are much speculated and I have spent many hours throughout many years pondering its origins with others. During the plantation days, *mamansan* referred either to the Buddha or to the altar in which the Buddha was housed. There was no clear distinction between the two. One thought is that the word somehow may have derived from the word *mamoru*, "to protect." Another thought is that it may have stemmed from Namu Amida Butsu, a Pure Land recitation expressing trust in Amida Buddha. Some wondered if when said quickly, "Nam'man'da, Nam'man'da," could've been misheard as *mamansan*. Yet another thought is that the word may have some connection with the clapping of the hands when praying.

The thought which I am favoring is that it comes from *manma*, the Japanese term used for "cooked rice" when speaking with children. Because it may be referring to the rice placed on the altar as an offering to the Buddha, the honorific *–san* may have been placed at the end of *manma* making it "the honorable rice," so to speak. As for the "n" in *manma* following the first "a" to the "n" following the second "a" in *maman*, it may be attributable to easier pronunciation or a "mis" of sorts.

I continue to relish in the contemplation regarding the origins of food-related terms and, as I do with actual food, enjoy it in the company of others.

✖ ✖ ✖

CHAPTER 11

Huh? What You Said?

The following stories shared with me are but glimpses of Hawai'i Plantation Pidgin in action as they reflect the communication of plantation days. They include examples of misunderstandings which can occur due to an amalgamation of words from different ethnic origins (The pretty what?) or misunderstandings of words which are similarly pronounced but from different origins and have different meanings (Speaking of flowers…). There is also the literal translation that doesn't quite translate the way we think it should with amusing consequences (The Golden Cat). The stories show the importance of the interconnectedness people feel with each other unaware the words they are using do not communicate since they are not from the origin of those whom they are addressing (Why Don't the Japanese in Japan Understand What I'm Saying?). Other stories capture the memories of school children and impart their non-discriminatory approach to language as they unknowingly share what they think are words of Japanese origin but which are actually of Hawaiian origin or vice-versa (Japanese School Memories). The anecdotal stories included here show how Japanese words can sound like English or how foreign words pronounced with a Japanese accent can become accepted as being Japanese. Finally, the *Obāchan* (Grandmother) Stories demonstrate the evolution of language being intergenerationally

shared while upholding, above all, the special bonds that can only be experienced between grandmother and grandchild.

The pretty what?

For a period of time, my dad worked as a caretaker for a state park. One day, while trimming some flowers, a tourist asked as to the kind of flowers they were. Not knowing, he replied, "*Me no sabe*," Pidgin for "I don't know." (English *me* [I] English *no* [don't] Portuguese *sabe* [know]). The tourist then turned to her companion and exclaimed, "Look at those pretty *menosabes*!"

Speaking of flowers…

A friend relayed the story of a discussion her grandfather was having with the family. He said "*Ano ohana o ki o tsukete*" which the family interpreted as "Take care of that flower." (Japanese *ano* [that], *ohana* [flower], *o ki o tsukete ki* [take care of]) Her cousin was ready to go into the garden to find out which flower needed such special attention. However, it was explained the word *'ohana*, in this case, was not being used as the Japanese word for "flower" but as the Hawaiian word for "family." What grandfather really meant was "Take care of that family." As they all learned, it referred to a family for which her grandfather was caring.

The Golden Cat

Tama (ball; gem) appeared to us in Hawai'i as a common Japanese name for a cat. So when a golden tabby entered into the life of my husband as a young child, he carefully considered an appropriate name. *Kin*, the Japanese word for "gold or golden" seemed the perfect descriptor to add to *Tama* resulting in the name, *Kintama*. After proudly announcing the new name for the cat, he was puzzled as to why his family objected to it. Unfortunately for the young child, he did not know that *kintama* was the Japanese word for "testicles."

Why Don't the Japanese in Japan Understand What I'm Saying?

While visiting a company she dealt with in Japan, a Hawai'i businesswoman saw a worker struggling with a task and offered to help. Her query of "*Kokuashite agemashōka*," however, was left unanswered. Although *~shite agemashōka* in Japanese is an offer to do whatever the verb that precedes it indicates, the word *kokua* (the Pidgin pronunciation of *kōkua*) had yet to be recognized in Japan as the Hawaiian word for help. In Hawai'i, *kōkua* is an oft used word as it reflects the culture of support and working together. *Kokua ni ike,* "go help," or *kokua shinasai,* "be of help," were commonly heard by children of the plantations as their parents instilled the values of cooperation and honor.

A friend's mother went to visit relatives in Japan bringing some candies with her for the children. When she saw them, she excitedly called to them and said, "*Girl-san, boy-san, kyande yaru*" meaning "Girl, boy, I will give you candy." However, the children continued playing with no response. Her mother probably didn't realize that excepting for *yaru* meaning "to give" there was no other Japanese word in the sentence.

After going back to Japan, a friend's uncle greeted someone he hadn't seen for a long time with "*Yo' tō machi makule nē*" which failed to elicit a response. Essentially, he was telling his friend, "You really aged." (English *yo* [you] English *tō machi* [too much] Hawaiian *makule* [aged] Japanese *nē* [particle *ne* used at the end of sentences is usually checking the agreement by the listener].)

Another friend's uncle went back to Japan and tried to tell someone that they had become fat. He used the word *momona* not realizing it was the Hawaiian word for "fat."

Japanese School Memories

A Japanese School teacher asked students what "orange" was in Japanese. One girl replied *alani*. The teacher then asked what part of Japan was she from. She didn't realize *alani* is the Hawaiian word for "orange."

A friend shared a similar experience at Japanese School. She said, "When I went to Japanese School, the teachers couldn't speak much English. And I was so proud when the *sensei* (teacher) asked what "friend" was because I knew. I raised my hand and said, "*Aikane*" to which he replied, "No, that's not it." I told him my *baban* (grandmother) said it was, and if she said it, it must be. I didn't know it was a Hawaiian word."

When asked what "finished" was by a Japanese school teacher, my friend replied *"Pau"* since she always heard her grandparents using it. She was very offended, as offended as a five-year old could be, when she was told it wasn't Japanese. It wasn't until she was in her teens that she learned it was a Hawaiian word.

On the other hand, a former Paʻauilo resident's experience was slightly different. He thought *bangō* was a Pidgin word until he went to Japanese School and found out it was standard Japanese for "number." He always thought it was Pidgin and derived from a combination of non-Japanese words.

Anecdotal Stories

Wakaran

Two *haole* (Caucasian) salesmen go to the plantation manager's or, I'm guessing more likely, the independent contractor's house who happens to be Japanese. His mother comes out and they ask her, "Can we see your son?" She looks at them and says, *"Wakaran"* meaning "I don't know" because she doesn't understand English and doesn't know what they're saying. Fifteen minutes later they come back and ask her again. She looks at them and again says, *"Wakaran"* because she still doesn't know what they're talking about. When they go the third time, her son is home. He tells them, "Oh, I just came home. This was good timing on your part. " And they reply, "No, we've been here for awhile." Curious, he asks, "What were you doing?" They replied, "Oh, we were listening to what your mother told us to do, we were walking around."

Oru men come kaukau pau hana hana

A lady returns home to the farm in Japan. It's lunchtime so she calls out the door, *Oru men come kaukau pau hana hana."* She waits awhile but nobody comes. Thinking they didn't hear her, she calls to them again even louder, "*Oru men come kaukau pau hana hana.*" Some of them look up but they still continue working. She couldn't understand why no one came, but unfortunately, she didn't realize she spoke not one word of Japanese so it was natural that they didn't understand her. (English *oru* [all] English *men come* [men come] Hawaiian *kaukau* [eat] *pau*[finish] *hana hana* [work] which translates to *Everyone, it's time to eat. Work time is finished.*)

Obāchan (Grandmother) Stories

A friend gave birth to a son whom she named "Darin." Excited to let her *obāchan* know what name was chosen, she carefully wrote his name in *katakana* (angular Japanese syllabary used primarily for loanwords). *Obāchan* commented on how it was such a popular name used by *haoles* when they called their loved ones "darling."

As one friend discovered, the generations, like the language, flow into each other and what may seem obvious is often only one person's perception. When her grandmother came to stay over, she could always count on her coming into the living room to tell her, "*Baban to moimoi.*" She didn't realize until years later as she was talking to her mother that her grandmother's *to* was the Japanese version meaning "with" and her grandmother was really asking her if she was going to sleep with her. She just assumed it was the Japanese pronunciation of the English word "to" and wondered why her grandmother looked so sad as she went off to bed without granddaughter in tow. Of course, as it is with grandparents and grandchildren, all was forgiven when she did go and cuddle with grandmother in bed.

And speaking of generations, a *sansei* woman living on the Mainland always spoke with her grandmother in Hawai'i. She had some difficulty understanding what she thought was Japanese only to later discover that it was not the Japanese of Japan but of Hawai'i. Yes, it was Hawai'i Plantation Pidgin—the Japanese Way!

Glossary

Note: Words containing the *kahakō* are alphabetized assuming its elongated sound as a double vowel. Therefore, *hānai (haanai)* precedes *haji* and *on* precedes *ōkī (ookii)*. Should the elongated *o* sound be considered a *u* which is common when Romanizing Japanese words, the word is alphabetized using the appropriate letter, that is to say, either the *o* or the *u*.

Word	Origin	Definition
abóbora	Portuguese	pumpkin
aikane	Hawaiian, from *aikāne*	friend; friendly
akan	Japanese, from *akemasen*	cannot open
ʻalani	Hawaiian	any kind of orange, both fruit and tree; orange color
anpan	Japanese	bread roll filled with bean paste
araimo	Japanese (*satoimo* in standard Japanese)	dasheen
atama	Japanese	head
ʻauʻau	Hawaiian	to bathe
(o)bāchan/ baban	Japanese	grandmother
bambai also bumbai	Pidgin, from English	by and by; later on

Word	Origin	Definition
bangō	Japanese	Adopted from the Japanese word for "number," *bangō* referred to the system and to the numbers themselves which identified workers on the plantations.
ben	Japanese	dialect (geographically specific)
(o)bentō	Japanese	Japanese box lunch
big(g)u shotto	Pidgin, from English (pronounced with a Japanese accent)	big shot
bobo (head)	Portuguese	fool; silly; idiot; imbecile; stupid
bocha	Pidgin, from Japanese onomatopoetic word for "splashing sound"	bath; bathe
(o)bon	Japanese	religious observance to honor one's ancestors (*Bon odori* or *bon* dances are traditionally included as part of the observance.)
bōbura	Japanese, derived from Portuguese, *abóbora*	pumpkin
bosh men	Pidgin, from English (pronounced with a Japanese accent)	boss man
bumbi also bumbbi	Pidgin, from English	by and by; later on

Word	Origin	Definition
bumby also bum by	Pidgin, from English	by and by; later on
bumbye also bum bye	Pidgin, from English	by and by; later on
bushi	Japanese, from *fushi*	song; melody; tune
chanoyu	Japanese (*sadō* in standard Japanese)	tea ceremony
chawan cut	Pidgin, from Japanese *chawan* for *rice bowl* and English *cut*	a haircut which looks like it resulted from a *chawan* being placed upside down on the head
choke	Pidgin	plenty
chōchi chōchi	Japanese	the first line in an interactive game played with babies
chōchin	Japanese	paper lantern
chow	Chinese	food
chūgi	Japanese	loyalty; devotion
cock-a-roach/ cockaroach see also kakaruch	English	cockroach
daimyo	Japanese	Japanese feudal lord in the Edo or Tokugawa period, 1803-1868
dango	Japanese	dumpling
doro	Japanese	mud
dorobo	Japanese, from *dorobō*	thief
eiyo	Japanese	honor

Word	Origin	Definition
English school	English	refers to public school where the curriculum was taught in English, used as a differentiation from Japanese school
erai	Pidgin, from Japanese	tired
erai	Japanese (standard)	great; excellent; admirable; remarkable; distinguished
gaijin	Japanese	foreigner
gaji	Pidgin, origin unknown	lightning card in the game, hanafuda; serves as the wild card
gaman	Japanese	perserverance
ganbari	Japanese	endurance
gannen	Japanese	first year of a specific reign
gannen mono	Japanese	first year people (When addressing the emigration of the Japanese to Hawai'i, it refers to the people of the first year of the Meiji Era.)
garans/ garans ballbarans	Pidgin, from English	guarantee(d)
garoot	origin unknown (May have derived from *galoot* which is also of unknown origin; first known use circa 1818.)	Commonly referred to in Hawai'i as go-fer (a person whose job is to do various small and usually boring jobs for other people). Galoot is defined as "a man or boy especially one who is foolish or awkward." Originally in nautical use meaning 'an inexperienced marine.'

Word	Origin	Definition
giri	Japanese	sense of duty; honor
girigiri	Pidgin, origin unknown	cowlick
girigiri	Japanese (standard)	at the last moment; just barely
gisei	Japanese	sacrifice
gosei	Japanese	fifth generation of Japanese descent; children of the *yonsei*
hānai	Hawaiian	foster child; adopted child
haji	Japanese	shame
hana/ hana hana	Hawaiian	work; labor
hana	Japanese	flower
hana	Japanese	nose
hanabata	Pidgin, from Japanese *hana* and English *butter*	nasal discharge (refers to liquid nasal mucus in Hawai'i)
hanafuda	Japanese	Japanese floral playing cards (12 suits of 4 cards, each suit represents a month indicated by a plant) While there are different games played in Japan, Korea, Micronesia and Hawai'i, the game *sakura* is specific to Hawai'i.
hanakuso	Japanese	nasal discharge (refers to dried nasal mucus in Hawai'i)
haole	Hawaiian	White person, American, Englishman, Caucasian; formerly, any foreigner (The original term, *hā'ole*, meant without breath or no life.)

Word	Origin	Definition
hapai/happai	Hawaiian, from *hāpai*	to carry, bear, life elevate, raise, hoist hold up; pregnant or to conceive
hapai hara/ happai hara	Pidgin, from Hawaiian *hāpai* and English *harrow*	to carry the harrow or plow, as formerly done by plantation workers
hapai ko/ happai ko	Hawaiian, from *hāpai kō*	to carry sugar cane bundles on the back, as formerly done by plantation workers
(o)hara	Japanese	abdomen; belly; stomach
hemo	Hawaiian	loose; separated; untied; unfastened; open
heso no goma	Japanese	belly button lint (Japan)
hesokuso	Japanese	belly button lint (Hawaiʻi)
hinoshi	Japanese	iron, as in ironing clothes
hippari men	Pidgin, from Japanese *hipparu* and English *men*	From the Japanese *hipparu*, to pull, the *hippari men* were the younger, stronger workers who were hired to set artificially faster paces for their fellow workers.
hoe hana	Pidgin, from English *hoe* and Hawaiian *hana*	Originally meaning doing hoe work in the cane fields, it is now used as a general term of doing work with a hoe such as digging or weeding in the yard or garden.
holehole	Hawaiian	to skin, peel, file, rasp make a groove; to strip, as sugar cane leaves from the stalk

Word	Origin	Definition
holehole bushi	Pidgin, from Hawaiian *holehole* and Japanese *bushi*	songs composed by immigrant Japanese workers which reflected the hardship, suffering and uncertainty of their life in Hawai'i
honohono	Hawaiian	The Wandering Jew or Dayflower *(Commelina diffusa)*
hōgen	Japanese	dialect
hōsenko	Japanese, from *hōsenka*	Garden Balsam *(Impatiens balsamina)*
ikebana	Japanese	flower arrangement
iran	Japanese, from *irimasen*	not needed
issei	Japanese	first generation of Japanese descent; immigrant from Japan
izakaya	Japanese	a casual drinking establishment
jabon	Japanese, from *zabon*	pomelo
jabu	Japanese, from onomatopoetic word for "splashing water sound"	bath; bathe
jan ken po	Japanese, from *jan ken pon*	a hand game played, usually by two people, to pass time or more often as a decision-making tool to determine an outcome
Jap	English	contraction for "Japanese"
jōzu	Japanese	skill; skillful; dexterity
(o)kāsan	Japanese	mother

Word	Origin	Definition
kaba	Japanese	hippopotamus; birch; cattail
kabocha	Japanese, for Cambodia derived from the Portuguese, *Cambodia abóbora*	pumpkin
kachi ken	Pidgin, from English (pronounced with a Japanese accent)	cut cane
kakaruch/ kakaroach see also cock-a-roach	English	cockroach
kamapio aka alapio, kamepio, kanapio, okamapio	Hawaiian	A game similar to American baseball in which either a branch or a broomstick approximately twenty inches is used as the bat and a shorter stick approximately six inches sharpened on both ends is used as the ball. It is this short stick that is called *pio.*
kansha	Japanese	gratitude
karinkarin	Pidgin, origin unknown	onomatopoetic sound of the bicycle bell
katakana	Japanese	angular Japanese syllabary used primarily for loan words

Word	Origin	Definition
kaukau	Hawaiian	Formerly a long mat on which food was placed; or from *pākaukau* meaning table, counter, stand, booth, desk. Currently used as a noun meaning "food" or as a verb to "come eat."
ken	Japanese	prefecture of Japan
kimono	Japanese	traditional Japanese clothing
kin	Japanese	gold; golden
kintama	Japanese	testicles
ko	Hawaiian, from *kō*	sugar cane *(Saccharum officinarum)* brought to Hawaiʻi by early Polynesians as a source of sugar and fiber. The thick stems are full of sweet juicy pulp. In time, many different kinds of cane were produced, with many different attributes and names.
kodomo	Japanese	child; children
kodomo no tame ni	Japanese	for the sake of the child(ren)
kokua	Hawaiian, from *kōkua*	help; aid; assistance
kompa(n[g])	Pidgin, from English companion (pronounced with a Filipino accent)	Originally meaning sugar cane cultivation by a small group who shared work together, *kompa(n[g])* has come to embrace the spirit of sharing as a way of life on the plantation, both at work and in the community. It is also a type of drinking gathering in Japan.

Word	Origin	Definition
kukui	Hawaiian	candlenut tree (*Aleurites moluccana*) A large tree in the spurge family bearing nuts containing white, oily kernels which were formerly used for lights, hence, the tree is a symbol of enlightenment.
kuso	Japanese	excrement
kyande	English (pronounced with a Japanese accent)	candy
liʻiliʻi	Hawaiian	here and there, piecemeal, a little at a time; small, little, in bits, diminutive, infantile, few; to scatter or fall in every direction
liliko/kolili	Pidgin, from Hawaiian *liʻiliʻi* and *kō*	piece(s) of cane left after being hand-cut or mechanically harvested; small cane; people who picked up the cane after it fell off the truck
lua	Hawaiian	toilet, outhouse, bathroom; cellar
luna	Hawaiian	foreman; boss; leader; overseer; supervisor
Mainland/ mainland	Pidgin, from English	contiguous United States
makule	Hawaiian	aged; elderly; old (of people)
mamankibi/ manmankibi	Japanese	corn

Word	Origin	Definition
mamansan/ manmansan	Japanese	During plantation days, *mamansan/manmansan* referred either to the Buddha or to the altar in which the Buddha was housed.
mamoru	Japanese	to protect; to guard; to defend
manma	Japanese	cooked rice
mata	Japanese	fork, as in a tree, road, river, etc.
mauka	Hawaiian	toward the mountains
mein	Chinese	noodle
mekuso	Japanese	eye discharge or mucus
menpachi	Pidgin, origin unknown	Fish belonging to the Holocentridae family. The subfamily Holocendtrinae is typically know as squirrelfish, while the members of the Myripristinae are typically known as soldierfish. In Hawai'i, they are known as *menpachi* or *'ū'ū* (Hawaiian).
mikan	Japanese	mandarin orange
mimikuso	Japanese	earwax
mizuna	Japanese	*Brassica rapa* var. *nipponsinica*
mochi	Japanese	rice cake
moimoi	Hawaiian, from *moemoe*	to sleep
momona	Hawaiian	fat
moyashi	Japanese	bean sprouts

Word	Origin	Definition
(o)musubi	Japanese	rice ball (*Musu* is based in Shintoism. It literally means to bring your hands together in front of you, touching them together in a clap symbolizing the joing of the gods, *Izanagi* [the male god] and *Izanami* [the female god]. When making rice balls, the hands are brought together in the same action.)
nisei	Japanese	second generation of Japanese descent; children of the *issei*
nomikai	Japanese	a drinking gathering phenomenon particular to the Japanese culture
odori	Japanese	dance
ʻohana	Hawaiian	family, relative, kin group; related
ojami/ojame	Japanese	Japanese game of *otedama* (beanbag)
on	Japanese	debt of gratitude
ōkī	Japanese	big
osechi	Japanese	traditional Japanese New Year's foods
oyakōkō	Japanese	filial piety
pākaukau	Hawaiian	table, counter, stand, booth, desk; formerly a long mat on which food was placed (*kaukau*)
Pake	Hawaiian, from *Pākē*	Chinese
pakiki	Hawaiian, from *paʻakikī*	hard, tough, unyielding; arbitrary, inflexible, compact, difficult, stubborn, obstinate

Word	Origin	Definition
pan	Portuguese, from *paó*	bread
pancit	Filipino	noodles
papale	Hawaiian, from *pāpale*	hat; head covering
papio	Hawaiian, from *pāpio*	same as *pāpiopio*. The young stage of growth of *ulua*, giant trevally, a species of large marine fish classified in the jack family.
pau	Hawaiian	finished; ended; through; terminated; completed
Pidgin/ Pidgin English	Pidgin first appeared in print in 1850 and is believed to possibly be from the Chinese pronunciation of "business."	In linguistics, Pidgin refers to a new language that develops because of the need to communicate by speakers who do not share a common language. The English in Pidgin English denotes the primary language from which the Pidgin is derived.
pilau	Hawaiian	rot; stench; rottenness; dirty
pilau maile/ kukai maile	Hawaiian, from maile pilau	*Parderia scandens* formerly *Parderia foetida*
pio	Hawaiian	the ball in the game *kamapio*
pio	Hawaiian	extinguished or out, as a fire or light
pipi	Hawaiian	beef; cattle; ox
Podagee	Pidgin, from English	Portuguese
popolo/ polopolo	Hawaiian, from *pōpolo*	Black Nightshade (*Solanum nigrum*)

Word	Origin	Definition
pulapula	Hawaiian	seedlings, sprouts, cuttings, as of sugar cane
sabe	Portuguese	know
sai	Chinese	thin
saimin/ saimein	Pidgin	a type of noodle soup
sakura	Pidgin (in this usage), from Japanese	While *sakura* is a Japanese term meaning "cherry blossoms," its application to the card game, *hanafuda*, is unique to Hawai'i.
samurai	Japanese	warrior, especially military retainers of *daimyo* during the Edo or Tokugawa period, 1803-1868
sansei	Japanese	third generation of Japanese descent; children of the *nisei*
sato	Japanese, from *satō*	sugar
satokibi	Japanese, from *satōkibi*	sugar cane *(Saccharum officinarum)*
sekinin	Japanese	responsibility
shītake	Japanese	type of edible mushroom *(Lentinula edodes)*
shikataganai	Japanese	resigned acceptance of a situation because it can't be helped but be that way
shin	Japanese	new
Shinto	Japanese, from *Shintō*	indigenous religion of Japan, translated to "The Way of the Gods"
shishi	Japanese, from *oshikko*	urine, urination; to urinate
shōjin	Japanese	vegetarian cuisine

Word	Origin	Definition
shuga ken	Pidgin, from English (pronounced with a Japanese accent)	sugar cane *(Saccharum officinarum)*
soba	Japanese	Japanese buckwheat noodles
(o)sonae	Japanese	offering
sumō	Japanese	sport of wrestling in Japan whose origins are based in the *Shintō* religion
takenoko	Japanese	bamboo shoots
talk story	Pidgin expression	informal chat; to chat informally
tama	Japanese	ball; gem
tamago	Japanese	egg
Timoshenko	Russian	surname of Ukranian origin
uekibi	Japanese	System that contracted group of laborers to cultivate a section of cane which organized itself, without a *luna,* managing the work process on its own.
ueru	Japanese	to plant; to grow
uhu	Hawaiian	the parrot fishes, of which Scarus perspicllatus is among the most abundant and largest
uke	Japanese	to contract; to undertake
ukepau	Pidgin, from Japanese *uke* for "contract" and Hawaiian *pau* for "finished"	agreed upon work quotas for the day
ukupau	Hawaiian	piece labor, pay by the job rather than according to time, as on sugar plantations

Word	Origin	Definition
wai wai	Hawaiian, from doubling of wai meaning "water" or "to flow, like water"	bath; bathe
wakaran	Japanese, from wakarimasen	(I) don't understand.
Yamato-damashī	Japanese	the spirit reflecting the native values of the Japanese, differentiating them from the values of foreign nations
yasai	Japanese	vegetables
yen	Japanese	Japan's present currency system which was established in 1871
yonsei	Japanese	fourth generation of Japanese descent; children of the *sansei*
yukata	Japanese	light cotton *kimono*
(o)zōni	Japanese	aka *mochi* soup, a New Year's dish of *mochi* cooked with vegetables

"Broken" English? Not!

One of the best answers I heard to the question as to whether Pidgin English is "broken" English is "No sta' broke, bugga' work fine." which essentially translates to "No, it (Pidgin English) is not broken, it works fine so it doesn't need any fixing."

The following pages are the culmination of not only my experiences but that of others who grew up in the Hawai'i Plantation Pidgin culture. Within these pages are the numerous interviews first conducted in the mid-1970s and still continues today; investigations and explorations through archives, museums, resource and cultural centers; research through books, articles, academic papers and journals—in hard copies as well as online; and by attending presentations which included both multiple participants and individuals. These activities are still ongoing in America as well as in Japan. As with the rest of the book, this part could only be written because of everyone's willingness to share the legacy of Hawai'i Plantation Pidgin.

As I mentioned in the Introduction, the word *erai* set me on this journey. After speaking with many people and collecting words and phrases they used on the plantations, the different categories which reflected the way that the Japanese spoke began to reveal themselves. These categories are simply my observations and are not in any way meant to be a linguistic account of any kind. Some categories are a lot more extensive than others but nonetheless each is distinct. The speech in some categories do indeed sound as though they may be "broken" but make no mistake, they are not. In fact, rather than being "broken," they served as the foundation for the communication which helped build and forge the strong bonds among the people on the plantations.

Let me now share with you in the Appendices the categories I found distinctive of the local Japanese speech which reflect Hawaiʻi Plantation Pidgin—The Japanese Way. These word lists contain both often heard phrases as well as those which may be unique to its speaker.

Appendix A

Appendix A consists of "Words Used and/or Said Differently When Compared with Standard Japanese" and encompasses the following types of words.

1. Those that are from geographical dialects, many from the Chūgoku region on the main island of Honshū, particularly Hiroshima. Words include *itashī* for *muzukashī* (hard; difficult), *miyasui* for *yasashī* (easy) and *taigī* for *tsukareta* (tired). There are words such as *sekarashī* for *yakamashī/ urusai* (annoying; noisy; irritating) which reflect dialects of other regions such as Kyūshū. The prolific use of words from these regions is not surprising since the Japanese population in Hawai'i by prefectural origin in 1924 showed that almost half were from the Chūgoku region and almost a quarter from Kyūshū.

2. Other words are those of shortened pronunciations such as *dako* from *dakko* (carry a baby in one's arms) and *marumoke* from *marumōke* (clear gain; profit) where a glottal stop or syllable is omitted.

3. Another grouping consists of words whose nuance may have changed from its original Japanese meaning. An example of this is *erai* whose accepted meaning in Hawai'i

is "tired" while its standard Japanese meaning is "great; excellent; admirable; remarkable; distinguished."

4. Other words included are those which still may be considered standard in Japan but are no longer used and are slipping into obscurity such as *anpontan* rather than *baka* for "fool or idiot," *benjo* rather than *otearai* or *toire* for "toilet" and *hinoshi* for *airon* as in ironing clothes.

"Phrases Used and/or Said Differently When Compared with Standard Japanese" are also included here since the same identifying markers used for "Words Used and/or Said Differently When Compared with Standard Japanese" are applicable.

✿　✠　✿

Japanese Words Used and/or Said Differently

Hawai'i Japanese Romanized	Hawai'i Japanese	Standard Japanese Romanized
anpontan	あんぽんたん	baka
ariko	ありこ	arinko
Note: *Children in Japan refer to ants as arinko. Adults call ants ari.*		
baiki	ばいき	ōmafubukuro;
		jyūto
banzai	万歳	kanpai
benjo	便所	otearai; toire
bento (bako)	べんと(箱)	bentō (bako)
bocha	ぼちゃ	ofuro ni hairu
chagai	ちゃがい	chagayu
chichi mochi	乳もち	gyūhi mochi
chingiru	ちんぎる	chongiru
chisha	ちしゃ	retasu
chitto	ちっと	sukoshi
dakkodakko	だっこだっこ (a feeling of love and affection is implied)	onbu
dako	だこ (a feeling of love and affection is implied)	dakko
dakochan	だこちゃん	ningyo

Standard Japanese	English	Part of Speech
バカ	fool; idiot	noun
あり	ant	noun
黄麻布袋; ジュート	bag (often a burlap bag)	noun
乾杯	a toast in celebration or in honor of something	noun
お手洗い; トイレ	toilet	noun
弁当 (箱)	Japanese box lunch (lunch box)	noun
お風呂に入る	take a bath; bathe (from Japanese onomatopoetic word for "splashing sound")	verb
茶粥	rice gruel with tea	noun
ぎゅうひ餅	a type of soft Japanese confectionery	noun
ちょん切る	snip (off); chop (off)	verb
レタス	lettuce	noun
少し	little; little bit (as in amount)	adj
おんぶ	piggyback (as to carry a baby on one's back)	noun
抱っこ	carry a baby in one's arms	verb
人形	doll	noun

Hawai'i Japanese Romanized	Hawai'i Japanese	Standard Japanese Romanized
darashiganai	だらしがない	darashinai
deko/dekochan	でこ/でこちゃん	ningyo
erai	えらい	tsukareta

Note: *In standard Japanese, erai is defined as great; excellent; admirable; remakable; distinguished.*

etto	えっと	takusan
futoi	ふとい	ōkī
girigiri	ぎりぎり	sakage

Note: *In standard Japanese, girigiri is defined as at the last moment or barely.*

habuteru	はぶてる	fukureru
hagamoge/ hagamuge	はがもげ/はがむげ	hanuke
hagemoge/ hagemuge	はげもげ/はげむげ	hanuke
hagemogi	はげもぎ	hanuke
hagaī	はがいい	iraira

Note: *The nuance of hagaī is that you've become frustrated because of someone else's action; whereas iraira refers to being irritated in a general sense.*

hantai	はんたい	gyaku
heka	へか	sukiyaki

Note: *Heka is often spelled hekka in Hawai'i.*

hichirin	ひちりん	shichirin
hinoshi	ひのし	airon
hoichō	ほいちょう	hōchō
hoitobo	ほいとぼ	yokubari
hōrokubaka	ほうろくばか	baka
hōsenko	ほうせんこ	hōsenka

Standard Japanese	English	Part of Speech
だらしない	sloppy; undisciplined	adj
人形	doll	noun
疲れた	tired	verb
たくさん	plenty	noun
大きい	big; fat	adj
逆毛	cowlick	noun
膨れる	to pout	verb; noun
歯抜け	toothless	adj
歯抜け	toothless	adj
歯抜け	toothless	adj
イライラ	frustrating, irritating	verb
逆	opposite	adj
すき焼	one pot dish	noun
七輪	charcoal brazier	adj
アイロン	iron (as in ironing clothes)	verb
包丁	kitchen knife	noun
欲張り	greedy	adj
バカ	fool; idiot	noun
ほうせんか	Garden Balsam (*Impatiens balsamina*)	noun

Hawai'i Japanese Romanized	Hawai'i Japanese	Standard Japanese Romanized	
inagena	いなげな	okashī; henna	

Note: *My mother used the term inagena kao when she felt I was either making an ugly face or an inappropriate expression. Another interpretation of inagena is nandemoī meaning trifling, nothing or of no concern.*

irankoto	いらんこと	tsumaranaikoto; yokeinakoto	
itashī	いたしい	muzukashī	

Note: *(Use of this term is obscure today) The nuance of itashī in Hawai'i is that you cannot say anything because the relationship you have with the person causes you to not say anything thereby causing you hardship.*

iyashī	いやしい	iyagaru	
jabon	じゃぼん	zabon	
jakuro	じゃくろ	zakuro	
kaī	かいい	kayui	
kishanai/ kichanai	きしゃない/きちゃない	kitanai	
kodomo taisho (from taishō)	子供対象; 子供大将	gakidaishō	
komai	こまい	chīsai	
kōkō/konkon	こうこう/こんこん	tsukemono	

Note: *In Hawai'i, it has come to mean tsukemono made from daikon.*

konaida	こないだ	konoaida	
koraejō	こらえじょう	koraeshō	
maderu	までる	mazeru	
mamankibi/ manmankibi	ままんきび/ まんまんきび	tōmorokoshi	
mamangoto/ manmangoto	ままんごと/まんまんごと	mamagoto	

Standard Japanese	English	Part of Speech
おかしい；　変な	weird; strange; odd; queer; ugly	adj
つまらない； 余計な事；	say or do unncessary things	adj
難しい	hard, difficult	adj
嫌がる	unpleasant	adj
ザボン	pomelo	noun
柘榴	pomegranate	noun
痒い	itchy; itching	adj
汚い	dirty	adj
ガキ大将	boss (leader) of the children	noun
小さい	small	adj
漬物	pickled vegetables	noun
この間	the other day; lately; recently	noun
堪え性	endurance; perseverance; patience	noun
混ぜる	to mix	verb
玉蜀黍	corn	noun
ままごと	play(ing) house	noun

Hawai'i Japanese Romanized	Hawai'i Japanese	Standard Japanese Romanized	
mamansan/ manmansan	ままんさん/まんまんさん	butsudan	

Note: *The origin of mamansan may have come from the Japanese word for cooked rice, manma. It was normal practice in many households that the fresh cooked rice before being consumed was always first offered to the Buddha. The term for the first offering is ohatsu which means the first.*

marumoke	まるもけ	marumōke	
mettaini	めったいに	mettani	
mimikuri	耳くり	mimikaki	
miyasui	みやすい	yasashī	
mofu	もふ	mōfu	

Note: *In Hawai'i, refers also to flannel or muslin.*

nachoran	なちょらん	baka	
nanashi gonbei	ななし ごんべい	nanashi no gonbē	
nashite	なして	dōshite; naze	
nasubi	なすび	nasu	
nigaharu	にがはる	ōgesa; hade	
ojami	おじゃみ	otedama	
okai	おかい	okayu	
oppa	おっぱ	onbu	
rankyō	らんきょう	rakkyō	
sekarashī	せからしい	yakamashī; urusai	

Note: *Those who used this term defined it as "busyness or nervous" in association with children, implying perhaps that the children's level of activity, or busyness, made one nervous.*

seki	セキ	byōki	
shinpai	しんぱい	omiai	

Standard Japanese	English	Part of Speech
仏壇	Buddhist altar (used in the home)	noun
丸儲け	clear gain; profit	noun
滅多に	rarely; seldom	adv
耳かき	ear pick	noun
易しい	easy	adj
毛布	blanket	noun
バカ	fool; idiot	noun
名無しの権兵衛	No Name (the American version of John Doe)	noun
どうして; なぜ	why	adv
茄	eggplant	noun
おおげさ; はで	extravagant (something is too good for the person); gaudy	adj
お手玉	(game of) bean bags	noun
お粥	rice gruel	noun
おんぶ	piggyback (as in carrying a child)	noun
らっきょう	Japanese leek	noun
やかましい; うるさい	annoying; noisy; irritating	adj
病気	sick	noun
お見合い	arranged marriage	noun

Hawai'i Japanese Romanized	Hawai'i Japanese	Standard Japanese Romanized
shishi	しし	oshikko
shitagi	したぎ	surippu
taigī	たいぎい	tsukareta

Note: *The nuance of "tired" as used here implies being tired of something or someone rather than physically.*

Hawai'i Japanese Romanized	Hawai'i Japanese	Standard Japanese Romanized
tamana	たまな	kyabetsu
tantaran	たんたらん	baka
taransuke	たらんすけ	baka
tarantaran	たらんたらん	baka
teresuke	てれすけ	baka
uji	うじ	kimochi ga warui
umu nai	うむない	oishiku nai
waideni	わいでに	wariai
warabesuke	わらべすけ	sukebe
washa (from washi wa)	わしゃ(わしは)	Watashi wa
washi	わし(male)	watashi
washira	わしら	watashitachi
yosha	よしゃ	enryo
zeni	ぜに	okane

Standard Japanese	English	Part of Speech
おしっこ	urine, urination; to urinate	noun; verb
スリップ	slip (as in undergarment)	noun
疲れた	tired	adj
キャベツ	cabbage	noun
バカ	fool; idiot	noun
バカ	fool; idiot	noun
バカ	fool; idiot	noun
バカ	fool; idiot	noun
気持ちが悪い	creepy (feeling)	adj
美味しくない	tasteless; not delicious	adj
割り合い	comparatively (more or less)	adv
スケベ	lecher	noun
私は	I (contraction form of pronoun when used with particle "wa")	pronoun
私	I; me	pronoun
私達	we; us	pronoun
遠慮	to be restrained or reserved	noun
お金	money (currency system used in Japan prior to yen)	noun

Japanese Phrases Used and/or Said Differently

Hawai'i Japanese Romanized	Hawai'i Japanese	Standard Japanese Romanized
Aitsura wa shiran nō.	あいつらはしらんのー 。	Ano hitotachi wa shiranai.
Asōde arimasuka?	あそうでありますか?	Sayōdegozaimasuka?
Dōka?	どうか?	Ikaga desuka?
Etto aru.	えっとある 。	Takusan arimasu.
Hara ga hetta.	はらがへった 。	Onakaga suiteimasu.
Itte kaerimasu.	いってかいります 。	Itte mairimasu./ Itte kimasu.
Jaman naru.	じゃまんなる.	Jama ni naru.
Jaman ni naru.	じゃまんになる.	Jama ni naru.
Komo ni kiru	こも(に 切る)	Komakaku (kiru)
Mamenaka?	まめなか?	Ogenki desuka?
Mamemaku?	まめまく?	Ogenki desuka?
Nanbo?	なんぼ?	Ikura desuka?
		Nansai desuka?
Sōde gansuka?	そうでがんすか?	Sōdegozaimasuka?
Yūkoto kikan.	ゆうこときかん 。	Iukoto o kikanai.

Standard Japanese	English
あの 人達 は 知らない。	They don't know.
さようでございますか?	Is that so? Really?
いかがですか?	How are you?
たくさんあります。	There's plenty.
お腹がすいています。	I'm hungry.
行ってまいります。/ 行ってきます。	I'm leaving (the house) now.
邪魔になる	To be an obstacle or hindrance; to
邪魔になる	get in the way
細かく(切る)	Cut into small pieces
お元気ですか?	How are you? (pertaining to health)
お元気ですか?	How are you? (pertaining to health)
いくらですか?	How much does it cost?/
何歳ですか?	How old (are you)?
そうでございますか?	Is that so?
言う事を聞かない。	You don't listen/(S)he doesn't listen.

Appendix B

The words in Appendix B, "Japanese Words, Phrases and Sentences Interjected with Other Languages," result from the influences and assimilation of languages of non-Japanese integrated with Japanese. Words such as *holehole bushi* (*holehole*, Hawaiian for "stripping dried sugar cane leaves from the stalk" and *bushi*, Japanese for "song or melody") in the chapter addressing plantation terms were created for easier communication regarding plantation work. Other words were created to express terms of everyday life such as *buta kaukau can* (*buta*, Japanese for" pig;" *kaukau*, Hawaiian for "food;" and *can*, English for "container") for "garbage can."

Japanese Interjected Words and Phrases

Hawai'i Japanese Romanized	Hawai'i Japanese	Standard Japanese Romanized
baka brain	ばかbrain	baka
baka lōlō	ばかlōlō	baka
bento tin	べんとtin	bentō bako
bobura head/ bobora head	ぼぶら/ぼぼら head	baka
buta kaukau	ぶたカウカウ	namagomi
buta kaukau can	ぶたカウカウ can	gomibako
chawan cut	ちゃわん cut	masshurūmu katto
chibitto	ちビット	sukoshi
chichi bando	乳バンド	bura; buraja
chittobit	ちっと bit	sukoshi
chittobitto	ちっと bitto	sukoshi
chottobit	ちょっとbit	sukoshi
ē boy	ええboy	ī otokonoko
hanabata	鼻バタ	hanamizu
hippari men	ひっぱり men	hipparu hito; hippari yaku
holehole bushi	holeholeぶし	nōsagyōka

Standard Japanese	English	Word Origin	Part of Speech
バカ(たれ)	stupid brain (stupid)	Jpnse/Eng	adj
バカ(たれ)	stupid, feeble-minded (stupid)	Jpnse/ Hawn	adj
弁当箱	lunch container	Jpnse/Eng	noun
バカ(たれ)	pumpkin head(stupid)	Port/Eng	adj
なまごみ	pig food (garbage, slop)	Jpnse/ Hawn	noun
ごみばこ	pig food can (garbage/ slop can/pail)	Jpnse/ Hawn/ Eng	noun
マッシュルーム カット	a style of haircut	Jpnse/Eng	noun
少し	small quantity; little; few	Jpnse/Eng	adj
ブラ; ブラジャ	bra	Jpnse/Eng	noun
少し	small quantity; little; few	Jpnse/Eng	adj
少し	small quantity; little; few	Jpnse/Eng	adj
少し	small quantity; little; few	Jpnse/Eng	adj
いい男の子	good boy	Jpnse/Eng	
鼻水	liquid nasal mucus	Jpnse/Eng	noun
引っ張る人; 引っ張り役	workers who were paid more to set artificially faster paces for their fellow workers	Jpnse/Eng	noun
農作業歌	Japanese plantation songs	Hawn/ Jpnse	noun

Hawai'i Japanese Romanized	Hawai'i Japanese	Standard Japanese Romanized	
hottsui/hotsui	hot つい/hotすい	atsui	
	(from つ→す)		
koppe yama	コッペ山	kōhī batake	

Note: *The reference to "mountain" may have come from the fields in Kona which were often located on mountain slopes.*

oku no camp	奥のcamp	oku no kyanpu	
shigoto men	仕事men	rōdōsha	
shita no camp	下のcamp	shita no kyanpu	
soda mizu	soda水	kōla	
sukoshi bit	少しbit	sukoshi	

Standard Japanese	English	Word Origin	Part of Speech
暑い	hot	Eng/Jpnse	adj
			noun
コーヒー畑	coffee mountain (coffee fields)	Hawn/Jpnse	noun
奥のキャンプ	(the) camp beyond	Jpnse/Eng	
労働者	workmen	Jpnse/Eng	noun
下のキャンプ	(the) camp below	Jpnse/Eng	
コーラ	soda water (soda)	Eng/Jpnse	noun
少し	small quantity; little; few	Jpnse/Eng	noun

Japanese Interjected Sentences

Hawai'i Japanese Romanized	Hawai'i Japanese	Standard Japanese Romanized	
Ano kanaka wa mī no aikane.	あの カナカ は mī の アイカネ。	Ano Hawaian wa watakushi no tomodachi desu.	

Note: "Me" was elongated to "mī" when pronounced by the Japanese immigrants.

Ano ohana ki o tsukete.	あの オハナ き を つけて。	Ano kazoku o daiji ni shite agete kudasai.	
Are wa lōlō ya.	あれは lōlō や。	Ano hito wa bakadesu.	
Ashita holoholo ikō.	明日 ホロホロ いこう。	Ashita dokoka e dekakemashō.	
Ay, you hemo kutsu.	Ay, you ヘモくつ。	Kutsu o nuide kudasai.	
Coffee waiteru yo.	Coffee わいてる よ。 (The coffee is boiled.)	Kōhī no yōi wa dekite imasu.	
Issho ni wai wai shinasai.	いっしょにワイ ワイ しなさい。	Issho ni ofuro ni hairinasai.	

Standard Japanese	English	Word Origin
あの ハワイアン は 　私 の 友達です。	That Hawaiian is my friend.	Jpnse: Ano; wa; no Hawn: kanaka; aikane
		Eng: me
あの 家族 を 大事 にして 　あげてください。	Take care of that family.	Jpnse: Ano; ki o tsukete Hawn: ohana
あの 人 はばかです。	That person is stupid.	Jpnse: Are wa; ya Hawn: lōlō
明日 どこか へ 　出かけましょう。	Let's go somewhere tomorrow./ Let's go on an outing tomorrow.	Jpnse: Ashita; ikō Hawn: holoholo
靴 を 脱いで 下さい。	Please remove your shoes.	Eng: Ay, you Hawn: hemo Jpnse: kutsu
コーヒー の 用意 は 　できています。	The coffee is ready.	Eng: Coffee Jpnse: waiteru yo
一緒にお風呂に 　入り なさい。	Go take a bath together.	Jpnse: Issho ni; shinasai Hawn: wai wai

Hawai'i Japanese Romanized	Hawai'i Japanese	Standard Japanese Romanized
Kaukau bai.	カウカウばい。	Gohan desu yo.
Kokua ni ike.	コクアにいけ	Tetsudai ni itte.
Kokua shinasai.	コクアしなさい。	Tetsudai nasai.
Kokua shite agemashōka.	コクアして あげましょうか。	Tetsudatte agemashōka?
Koppe nome.	コッペ飲め。	Kōhī o nonde; Kōhī wa jibun de dōzo.

While this phrase may sound like a command, its nuance, in actuality, is of a more polite nature. In the interest of saving time, messages often needed to be delivered as quickly, directly and in the shortest time possible. Therefore, political correctness was not a priority although, I believe, the warmth of the heart still emanated.

Light tsuketemo ē?	Light つけてもえー？	Denki tsuketemo yoroshī deshō ka?
Manuwahi mottekitara ē.	マヌワヒ持って来たら えー。	Tada de moraeba īyo nē.
Mauka fire, opu pilikia, down below shāshā.	マウカfire, オプ ピリキア, down below しゃーしゃー	Netsu ga atte, onaka mo itakute, geri mo shiteru.

Standard Japanese	English	Word Origin
ご飯ですよ。	Come eat.	Hawn: Kaukau Jpnse: bai
手伝いに行って	Go help. (command)	Hawn: Kokua Jpnse: ni ike
手伝いなさい	Be of help.	Hawn: Kokua Jpnse: shinasai
手伝って 　あげましょうか?	Can I help you?	Hawn: Kokua Jpnse: shite 　agemashōka
コーヒー を のんで; コーヒー は自分で どうぞ。	Drink coffee; Help yourself to coffee.	Hawn (pidginized): koppe Jpnse: nome
電気つけても 　よろしいでしょうか?	Is it alright to turn on the light?	Eng: Light Jpnse: tsuketemo ē
ただでもらえば 　いいよねー。	It's good if you can get it for free.	Hawn: manuahi Jpnse: mottekitara ē
熱があって、 　お腹もいたくて、 　下痢もしている。	(I have) a fever, 　stomach problems 　and diarrhea	Hawn; Mauka; opu pilikia Eng: fire; down below Jpnse: shāshā

Hawai'i Japanese Romanized	Hawai'i Japanese	Standard Japanese Romanized	
Mī mo no sabe.	Mī もno サベ。	Watakushi mo shirimasen.	

Note: *The use of "no" in this case is in place of the English "don't" and not as the Japanese possessive particle.*

My house ni konban kon ka?	My house に今晩に こんか？	Konban uchi e konai deshō ka?	
Wahine o yonda.	ワヒネを呼んだ。	Tsuma o yobiyosemashita.	
Wife morōta Japan kara.	Wife もろうた ジャパンから。	Tsuma o Nihon kara moraimashita.	
Yū kata mī kata Shōgatsu ni konkatta.	Yū かた mī かた正月に こんかった。	Anata (tachi) wa Oshōgatsu ni konakatta yo nē.	

Standard Japanese	English	Word Origin
私も知りません。	I, too, don't know.	Eng: Me; no Jpnse: mo Port: sabe
今夜うちへ来ない でしょか?	Won't you come to my house this evening?	Eng: My house Jpnse: ni konban kon ka
妻を呼び寄せました。	Called my woman (I called my wife).	Hawn: Wahine Jpnse: o yonda
妻を日本から もらいました。	I got my wife from Japan.	Eng: Wife; Japan (the immigrants pronounced the "a"s like the "a" in "father." Jpnse: morōta; kara
あなた(達)は お正月に 来なかったよねー。	You didn"t come to my house for the New Year party.	Eng: You; me Jpnse: kata; Shōgatsu ni konkatta

Japanese Interjected Prepositions

Hawai'i Japanese Romanized	Hawai'i Japanese	Standard Japanese Romanized	
mī ga	ミーが	watashi ga	
mī wa	ミーは	watashi wa	
mī no	ミーの	watashi no	
yū ga	ユーが	anata ga	
yū wa	ユーは	anata wa	
yū no	ユーの	anata no	
mī ra	*ミーら	wata(ku)shi tachi	
mī ra wa	*ミーらは	wata(ku)shi tachi wa	
yū ra	*youら	anata tachi	
yū ra wa	*youらは	anata tachi wa	
*Note: The "-ra" may be of Hiroshima origin since when referring to a group of individuals they put "-ra" at the end of pronouns or nouns.			

Standard Japanese	English	Part of Speech
私 が	I (followed by subject, topic and	noun
私 は	possessive particles)	noun
私 の		noun
あなた が	you (followed by subject, topic	noun
あなた は	and possessive particles)	noun
あなた の		noun
私達	we	noun
私達は	we (followed by topic particle)	noun
あなた達	you, you folks	noun
あなた達は	you, you folks (followed by topic particle)	noun

Appendix C

Appendix C, "Non-Japanese Words and Phrases Accepted and Adopted into Use as Japanese," are those words used by the Japanese as Japanese words although their origins were actually based in other languages. *Pau*, Hawaiian for "finished" and *tō machi*, English for "too much" are examples of these words.

Non-Japanese Words and Phrases Accepted as Japanese

Hawai'i Japanese Romanized	Hawai'i Japanese	Standard Japanese Romanized	Standard Japanese	
akamai	アカマイ	jōzu	じょうず	
auau	アウアウ	ofuro	お風呂	
bambai	バンバイ	nochihodo	のちほど	
Note: *Variant spellings include bumbai, bumbi (also bumbbi); bumby (also bum by); bumbye (also bum bye)*				
barato	バラト	osusowake	お裾分け	
big(g)u shotto	big(グ)ショット	taisetsu na hito	大切な人	
bosh men	boshメン	shihainin	支配人	
chiroi away	チロイaway	suteru	捨てる	
fōru	フォール	ochiru	落ちる	
guru boy	グルboy	ī otoko no ko	いい男の子	
hana/hana hana	ハナ/ハナ ハナ	shigoto	仕事	
hanawai	ハナワイ	mizu o ireru/haru (tanbo ni)	水を入れる/はる（田んぼに）	
hapai/happai	ハパイ/ハッパイ	hakobu	はこぶ (運ぶ)	
hapai go	ハパイゴ	hakonde iku	はこんでいく	
hapai hara	ハパイハラ	tagayasu	耕す	
hapaiko/happaiko	ハパイコ/ハッパイコ	~katsugu	〜担ぐ	

English	Word Origin	Part of Speech
smart; clever	Hawn	adj
to bathe	Hawn	verb
by and by/later; eventually	Eng	adv
giving extra; giving free; sharing wealth	Filipino from Spanish for "cheap"	adv/adj
big shot/important person	Eng	noun
boss man/boss; manager	Eng	noun
throw away	Eng	verb
fall	Eng	verb
good boy	Eng	noun
work	Hawn	verb
watering the cane(field); irrigate	Hawn	verb
to carry	Hawn from *hāpai*	verb
hapai go/to carry and go	Hawn: hāpai; Eng: go	verb
hapai hara/to carry the harrow (plow)	Hawn: hāpai and Eng: harrow	verb
hapai ko/happai ko/ to carry sugar cane bundles on the back	Hawn from *hapaikō*	verb

Hawai'i Japanese Romanized	Hawai'i Japanese	Standard Japanese Romanized	Standard Japanese	
hapa/happa	ハパ/ハッパ	konketsu	混血	
hemo	ヘモ	hazusu	外す	
hoe hana	ホハナ	horu	掘る	
holehole	ホレホレ	kawa o muku	皮をむく	
holoholo	ホロホロ	dekakeru	出かける	
kachiken	カチケン	karitoru	刈り取る	
kachiken knife	カチケンknife	kama	鎌	
kakio	カキオ	kanō	化膿	
kalakoa	カラコア	karafuru	カラフル	
kanaka	カナカ	Hawaiian/ Hawaii hito	ハワイアン/ ハワイ人	
kane	カネ	otto; dansei	夫; 男性	
kapulu	カプル	darashinai	だらしない	
karabōshi	カラボーシ	rōya	牢屋	
karu	カル	kuruma	車	
kaukau	カウカウ	tabemono/ taberu	食べ物/食べる	
kaukau can	カウカウ can	bentō bako	弁当箱	
kaukau tin	カウカウ tin	bentō bako	弁当箱	
kolohe	コロヘ	itazura	いたずら	
kompa(n[g])	コンパ/ コンパン	wakeau	分け合う	

English	Word Origin	Part of Speech
person of mixed ethnicity; biracial	Hawn	noun
take off; remove	Hawn	verb
to do work with a hoe such as digging, weeding	Eng: hoe and Hawn: hana	verb
to strip, as sugar cane leaves from the stalk	Hawn	verb
go on an outing	Hawn	verb
to cut cane	Eng	verb
cane knife	Eng	noun
pustules (sores)	Hawn	noun
variegated in color; colorful	Hawn	adj
Hawaiian (person)	Hawn	noun
husband; male	Hawn from kāne	noun
careless; slovenly; undisciplined	Hawn from *kāpulu*	adj
calaboose/prison	Eng from Spanish	noun
car	Eng	noun
food; eat	Hawn	noun/ verb
lunch can	Hawn: kaukau; Eng: can	noun
lunch can	Hawn: kaukau; Eng: tin	noun
mischievous; naughty	Hawn	adj
share	English from the Filipino pronunciation of "companion"	verb

Hawai'i Japanese Romanized	Hawai'i Japanese	Standard Japanese Romanized	Standard Japanese
koppe	コッペ	kōhī	コーヒー
lili bit	リリbit	sukoshi dake	少しだけ
lili mo'	リリモ	mō sukoshi	もう少し

Note: Although "mō'" may be derived from either the English "more" or the Japanese "mō," the consensus among those with whom I spoke believe it is the derivative from the English "more." This conclusion may be the result of the context in how it is used. That is to say, "little more" pronounced with a Japanese accent might be more natural in speech given its particular context rather than using a combination of English "little" and Japanese "mō" although I cannot say for certain that it is a forgone conclusion given the dynamics of Hawai'i Plantation Pidgin.

liliko/kolili	リリコ/コリリ	karinokoshi	刈り残し
luna	ルナ	nōjō no kantokusha	農場の監督者
makai	マカイ	umi no hō	海の方
make, die, dead	マケ、ダイ、dead	tashikani shinde imasu	確かに死んでいます
makule	マクレ	nenpai	年配
mauka	マウカ	yama no hō	山の方
Meriken	メリケン	America	アメリカ
mo' bettah	モベター	Kono hō ga ii.	この方がいい
moimoi	モイモイ	neru	寝る
momona	モモナ	futtote iru	太っている
mon picha	モンピチャ	eiga	映画

English	Word Origin	Part of Speech
coffee; coffee beans	Hawn from *kope*	noun
little bit/just a little	Eng	adj
little more/in a little while	Eng	adj
piece(s) of cane left after being hand-cut or mechanically harvested; small cane; people who picked up the cane after it fell off the truck	Hawn from *liʻiliʻi* (bits or to scatter) and *kō* (sugar cane)	
plantation overseer	Hawn	noun
toward the ocean	Hawn	noun
really, really dead	Hawn: make; Eng: die; dead	adj
aged; elderly (of people)	Hawn	adj/noun
toward the mountains; upland	Hawn	noun
America	Hawn	noun
more better/better	Eng	adj
to sleep; to sleep with someone (to have sex with someone)	Hawn from *moemoe*	verb
fat	Hawn	adj
motion picture/movie(s)	Eng	noun

Hawai'i Japanese Romanized	Hawai'i Japanese	Standard Japanese Romanized	Standard Japanese	
mon picha house	モンピチャ house	eigakan	映画館	
moroha	モロハ	namakemono	なまけもの	
nō guru	ノーグル	dame	ダメ	
o sem/oru sem	オsem/オル sem	onaji (yō)	同じ(よう)	
ōru men	オールメン	minna	皆	
ōtambīru	オータンビール	kuruma	車	
otombiru	オトンビル	kuruma	車	
Pake	パケ	Chūgokujin	中国人	
pakiki	パキキ	ganko	頑固	
papā	パパー	kogeru	焦げる	
papale	パパレ	bōshi	帽子	
pau	パウ	sumu; owaru	済む; 終る	
pilau	ピラウ	kitanai	きたない	

Note: *The often accepted meaning and use of pilau by many Japanese in Hawai'i is dirty (lepo in Hawaiian). Pilau also means rot; stench; rottenness; to stink; spoiled; rotten; foul; decomposed which are the actual definitions of the word.*

pio	プイ	kesu	けす	
pio shut	プイshut	kesu	けす	
pohō	ポホー	mottainai	もったいない	

English	Word Origin	Part of Speech
motion picture house/movie theatre	Eng	noun
lazy; indolent	Hawn from *moloā, molowā*	adj
no good/not good; bad	Eng	adj
all same/same; (just) like; similar to	Eng	adj
all men/everyone	Eng	noun
automobile/car	Eng	noun
automobile/car	Eng	noun
Chinese	Hawn from *Pākē*	noun
obstinate; hard-headed	Hawn from *paʻakikī*	adj
burnt	Hawn from *pāpaʻa*	verb
hat	Hawn from *pāpale*	noun
finished; ended; through; terminated; completed	Hawn	verb
dirty; rotten	Hawn	adj
extinguished or out, as in a fire or light	Hawn	verb
extinguished or out, as in a fire or light	Hawn:pio; Eng: shut	verb
loss; damage; wasteful	Hawn	adj

Hawai'i Japanese Romanized	Hawai'i Japanese	Standard Japanese Romanized	Standard Japanese	
pupule (pūpule is sometimes used for emphasis)	ププレ (プープレ)	kurējī	クレージー	

Note: *During plantation days, the term kichigai was used as the accepted Japanese term to mean crazy. However, in Japan today it is a considered a vulgar term and is not used by the ordinary person. Rather, terms describing the situation will be used. For instance, abunai (dangerous) would be used when someone is doing something risky or baka (fool; idiot) if someone is doing something which is considered stupid.*

Sande	サンデ	Nichiyōbi	日曜日
shaburu	シャブル	shaberu	シャベル
terebijen	テレビジェン	terebi	テレビ
terebijon	テレビジョン	terebi	テレビ

Note: *This term is accepted today in standard Japanese although its contracted form テレビ is more commonly used.*

terehon	テラホン	denwa	電話
tō machi	トーマチ	ōsugiru	多すぎる
ukupau	ウクパウ	teshigoto	手仕事
wahine	ワヒネ	josei; tsuma	妻; 女性)
wai wai	ワイ ワイ	ofuro	お風呂
washi	ワシ	sentaku	洗濯

English	Word Origin	Part of Speech
crazy; insane; reckless	Hawn (probably derived from pule, prayer)	adj
Sunday	Eng	noun
shovel	Eng	noun
television	Eng	noun
television	Eng	noun
telephone	Eng	noun
too much	Eng	noun/ adj
piece labor	Hawn	noun
wife; woman	Hawn	noun
to bathe (from water; to flow like water)	Hawn	verb
wash/washing; laundry	Eng	verb

Non-Japanese Sentences Accepted as Japanese

Hawai'i Japanese Romanized	Hawai'i Japanese	Standard Japanese Romanized	
Me no sabe.	Me no サベ.	(Watakushi wa) shirimasen.	
My shaburu fallu down ditch.	My シャブルファル down ditch.	Supūn wa yōsuiro ni ochite shimaimashita.	
No cabesa.	No カベサ.	Baka.	
No go alanui.	No go アラヌイ.	Dōro ni ikanaide.	
Oru men come kaukau, pau hana hana.	オルメン come カウカウ, パウ ハナ ハナ.	Minna shokuji ni shiyō. Shigoto wa owarimashita.	
pau hana/ pa' hana/ pau hana hana	パウ ハナ/パ ハナ/ パウ　ハナ ハナ	Shigoto ga owarimashita.	
You go (sta') go, bambai I go (sta') come.		Osaki ni dōzo. Tsuite ikimasu.	
Wassamata (you)?!		Dōshita no?	

Standard Japanese	English	Word Origin
(私 は) 知りません。	I don't know.	Eng: Me; no Port: sabe
スプーン は 用水路 に 落ちてしまいました。	My spoon fell in the flume.	Eng
バカ。	Not very intelligent (no brains).	Eng: No Spanish: cabeza (head)
道路に行かないで。	Don't go on the road.	Eng: No; go Hawn: alanui
みんな食事にしよう。 仕事は終わりました。	*All men* (everyone) come eat. Work time is finished.	Eng: all men come; Hawn: kaukau, pau hana hana
仕事 が 終わりました。	(I am) finished work/ Work is finished.	Hawn from pau (finished) and hana(work)
お先にどうぞ。 付いて行きま。	You go on ahead, I will come later.	Eng
どうしたの?	What's the matter (with you)?	Eng

Abbreviation of Word Endings

[A]

Standard ------>	Hawai'i
…りません→らん	り→ら drop ませ leave ん
…きません→かん	き→か dropませ leave ん
…みません→まん	み→ま drop ませ leave ん
…べません→べん	leave べ drop ませ leave ん
…けません→けん	leave け drop ませ leave ん

Note exception 1: きません→こん (carryover into Pidgin its irregularity in Japanese)

Note exception 2: かまりません→かまん rather than かまらん

Hawaii Japanese	Standard Japanese	English
いらん	いりません (いらない)	not needed
おらん	おりまっせん (おらない)	not here, not present
しらん	しりません (しらない)	don't know
たらん	たりません (たりない)	not enough
やらん	やりません (やりない)	won't give
こまらん	こまりません (こまらない)	no trouble
すわらん	すわりません (すわらない)	won't sit
つまらん	つまりません (つまらない)	no good
わからん	わかりません (わからない)	don't know (understand)

Hawaii Japanese	Standard Japanese	English
あかん	あけません	cannot open
いかん	いけません	cannot go
つかん	つけません	cannot go on, won't stick
やかん	やけません	cannot burn (cook)
のまん	のみません	won't drink
たべん	たべません	won't eat
あけん	あけません	can't open
やけん	やけません	can't fry (cook)

Irregular exceptions

Hawaii Japanese	Standard Japanese	English
こん	きません	won't come
かまん	かまりません	that's alright, not a problem

[B]

Standard	------>	Hawai'i
…いました		…うた

Hawai'i Japanese	Standard Japanese	English
こうた	かいました	bought
ゆうた	いいました	said
もろうた	もらいました	received

[C]

Standard	------->	Hawai'i
C.	…ましたか	…たんか
		…ったんか
		…んだんか
		…っしたんか

Hawaii Japanese	Standard Japanese	English
どうしたんか	どうしましたか	What happened?
見たんか	見ましたか	Did you (s/he) see it?
来たんか	来ましたか	Did s/he come?
できたんか	できましたか	Did you (s/he) do it?
行ったんか	行きましたか	Did you (s/he) go?
はいったんか	はきましたか	Did you (s/he) wear it?
はいったんか	はいりましたか	Did it fit/go in?
切ったんか	切りましたか	Did you (s/he) cut it?
おくったんか	おくりましたか	Did you (s/he) send it?
まわったんか	まわりましたか	Did it (you)(s/he) go around?
読んだんか	読みましたか	Did you (s/he) read it?
すんだんか	すみましたか	Did you (s/he) finish it?
けっしたんか	けしましたか	Did you (s/he) erase it?
おしったんか	おしえましたか	Did you (s/he) teach it?

[D]

Standard	------->	Hawai'i
D1.		…ですか
		…いんか

Hawai'i Japanese	Standard Japanese	English
いいんか	いいですか	Is it alright?
わるいんか	わるいですか	Is it bad?/Is the timing bad?

Standard	------->	Hawai'i
D2.		…ませんか
		…いんか

Hawai'i Japanese	Standard Japanese	English
ないんか	ありませんか	Do you have any?

[E]

Standard	------->	Hawai'i
E. …しますか		し➡す- ます replace with るん leave か
…りますか		り➡る- ます replace with ん leave か (result is still るんか as above)
…でいますか		-います replace with るん leave か
…きますか		き➡く-います replace with ん leave か
…ぎますか		ぎ➡ぐ- ます replace with ん leave か

Hawai'i Japanese	Standard Japanese	English
どうするんか	どうしますか	What shall we do?/ How shall we do it?
こうするんか	こうしますか	Are you going to do it like this?
するんか、せるんか	しますか	Are you going to do it?
あるんか	ありますか	Do you have any/it?
とるんか	とりますか	Are you going to take it?
だれよんでるんか	だれをよんでいますか	Who are you calling?
すんでるんか	すんでいますか	Are you finished?
どこおくんか	どこにおきますか	Where shall I put it?/Where are you going to put it?
泳ぐんか	泳ぎますか	Are you going to swim?
		Can't quite figure these out yet
着るんか	着ますか	Are you going to wear it?
すんだんか	すみましたか	Are you finished?
やねもりよるんだ	やねがもれています	The roof is leaking.

[F]

Standard	------->	**Hawaiʻi**
F. . . .なさい		. . .ない (command)

Hawaiʻi Japanese	**Standard Japanese**	**English**
食べない	食べなさい	Eat
行きない	行きなさい	Go
きない	来なさい	Come

[G]

Standard	------->	**Hawaiʻi**
G. . . .(ます)か		. . .け

Hawaiʻi Japanese	**Standard Japanese**	**English**
(バスまだ)くるけ	いつきますか	When will it (the bus) arrive?

[H]

Standard -------> Hawai‘i

H. . . .ています て➡と dropいます replace withる

       (May be an influence from Hiroshima-

       ben where―ている changes to―とる

       or―とく)

Hawai‘i Japanese	Standard Japanese	English
いきとる (いきてる)	いきています	(still) alive; live; exist
うえとる (うえてる)	うえています	planting; growing
おいとる (おいてる)	おいています	(left) at; in; on
なれとる (なれてる)	なれています	get used to
…わいてる	わいています	boiling
…ういてる	うきています	floating; non-attached

[I]

Standard -------> Hawai‘i

I1. . . .の   . . .ん

Hawai‘i Japanese	Standard Japanese	English
かざりもん	かざりもの	decoration, adornment

Standard -------> Hawai‘i

I2. . . .に   . . .ん

Hawai‘i Japanese	Standard Japanese	English
じゃまんなる	じゃまになる	get in the way

Standard -------> **Hawai"i**

13. . . .な . . .ん

Hawai'i Japanese	Standard Japanese	English
あんた	あなた	you

Bibliography

Books

Beechert, Edward D. *Working in Hawaii: A Labor History*. University of Hawai'i Press, 1985.

East Hawaii Cultural Center. *Aloha Aina: Big Island Memories*. 2012.

Hazama, Dorothy Ochiai. *Okage Sama De The Japanese in Hawaii* . Hawaii: Bess Press Inc., 1986.

Honma, Gaku. *The Folk Art of Japanese Country Cooking: A Traditional Diet for Today's World*. California: North Atlantic Books. 1993.

Horii, Reiichi. *Osaka Kotoba Jiten*. Tokyo: Tokyodo Publishing Company, 1995.

Japanese Women's Society of Honolulu and Japanese Women's Society Foundation. *Kokoro: Cherished Japanese Traditions in Hawaii*. Waipahu: Island Heritage, 2004.

Kaukali, Edwin L. and Subica, Wayne A. *Hawaii Plantations Pay System & History about the Old Days*. Hawaii: Memories of Hawaii—Big Island, LLC, 2nd ed. 2010.

Kimura, Yukiko. *Issei: Japanese Immigrants in Hawaii*. Honolulu: University of Hawai'i Press, 1988.

Kinoshita, Gaku. *Us, Hawaii-Born Japanese: Storied Identities of Japanese American Elderly from a Sugar Plantation Community*. New York and London: Routledge, 2006.

Kodama-Nishimoto, Michi, Nishimoto, Warren S., and Oshiro, Cynthia A. *Hanahana An Oral History Anthology of Hawaii's Working People*. Honolulu: University of Hawai'i Press, 1995.

Kotani, Roland. *The Japanese in Hawaii: A Century of Struggle.* Honolulu: The Hawaii Hochi, Ltd., 1985.

Kurisu, Yasushi "Scotch." *Sugar Town.* Honolulu: Watermark Publishing, 2000.

Laupahoehoe School. *April Fool's. . .The Laupahoehoe Tragedy of 1946.* Hawaii: Obun Hawaii, Inc.,1997.

Mattern, Joanne. *Japanese Americans (Immigrants in America).* New York: Chelsea House Publishers, 2003.

Miyamoto, Ted T. *Talk Story: Growing Up On A Sugar Plantation.* Nikkei Writers Guild A Division of Japanese American Living Legacy, 2010.

Odo, Franklin and Sinoto, Kazuko. *A Pictorial History of the Japanese in Hawaii 1885–1924.* Hawai'i Immigrant Heritage Preservation Center, 1985.

Odo, Franklin. *Voices from the Canefields.* New York: Oxford Press, 2013.

Ogawa, Dennis M. *Jan Ken Po.* Honolulu: Obun Printing Co., Inc., 1st ed. 1973.

Ogawa, Dennis M. and Grant, Glen. *To A Land Called Tengoku: One Hundred Years of the Japanese in Hawaii.* Honolulu: Mutual Publishing, 1985.

Okimoto, Tadao. *Onomea Camp, 1935, Hawaii.* T. Okimoto, A. Fujinaka: 1982.

Olaa Kurtistown 1996 . Oldtimers Reunion, July 12-13,1996.

Pukui, Mary Kawena, and Samuel H. Elbert. *Hawaiian Dictionary.* Honolulu: University of Hawai'i Press, 1986.

Sakoda, Kent and Siegel, Jeff. *Pidgin Grammar: An Introduction to the Creole Language of Hawaii.* Honolulu: Bess Press, Inc., 2003. (Printed in the United States of America)

Sato, Hiroo. *Pahoa.* Hilo, 2002.

Simonson, Douglas (Peppo) in collaboration with Sasaki, Pat and Sakata, Ken. *Pidgin to da Max.* Honolulu: Bess Press, 2005. (Printed in China)

Subica, Wayne A. *Hawaii Sugar Days.* Hilo: Memories of Hawaii—Big Island, LLC, 2013.

Takaki, Ronald T. *Pau Hana: Plantation Life and Labor in Hawaii, 1835-1920.* Honolulu: University of Hawai'i Press, 1983.

Tojo, Masao. *Zenkoku Hogen Jiten*. Tokyo: Tokyodo Publishing Company, 59th ed. 1995.

Tonouchi, Lee A. *Da Kine Dictionary*. Honolulu: Bess Press Inc., 2005. (Printed in Korea)

Newspaper Articles

"Na Paahana Iapana." *Ke Alaula*, 1 July 1868: Volume III, Number 4.

Ohira, Rod, "Waipahu Turns 100 One Sweet Century." *Star-Bulletin*, Honolulu, Hawaii. June 12, 1997: A-5.

Internet

http://classic.jisho.org/. Denshi Jisho – Online Japanese Dictionary.

http://clear.uhwo.hawaii.edu. University of Hawai'i – West O'ahu Center for Labor Education & Research, November 3, 2014.

http://en.numista.com/numisdoc/japan-51.html. Numista, Japan. November 4, 2014.

https://en.wikipedia.org/wiki/Japanese_currency. Japanese currency, July 24, 2014.

https://en.wikipedia.org/wiki/Konpa

https://en.wikipedia.org/wiki/Sansukumi-ken. Sansukumi-ken, June 27, 2015.

https://en.wikipedia.org/wiki/Saimin. Saimin, June 28, 2015.

https://en.wikipedia.org/wiki/Rock-paper-scissors. Rock-paper-scissors, July 15, 2014.

http:// hanafudahawaii.com/ginstructions.html. Hanafuda Hawaii Style, October 2, 2014.

http://publishing.cdlib.org/ucpressebooks/view?docId=ft9290090n&chunk. id=d0e378&t

oc.id=d0e373&brand=ucpress. University of California Press, UC Press E-Books Collection, 1982-2004. Japanese Immigration to Hawaii, March 10, 2013.

http://wehewehe.org. Nā Puke Wehewehe ʻŌlelo Hawaiʻi—ulukau Hawaiian Electronic Library.

http://www.ablelanguage.com/en/hiroshima-ben. Able Language Services Hiroshima Ben, April 24, 2013.

http://www.discovernikkei.org/en/nikkeialbum/albums/392/slide/?page=2. Young,

Nicole. Immigration: Japanese Arrival in Hawaii, November 5, 2014.

http://www.estat.us/id82.html. Hiroshima-ben World, April 13, 2013.

http://www.etymonline.com/. Online Etymology Dictionary, May 27, 2013.

http://www.jlect.com/entry/1432/boubura/. JLect Languages and dialects of Japan, June 7, 2015.

http://www.loc.gov/teachers/classroommaterials/presentationsandactivities/presentations/immigration/japanese.html. Library of Congress, Immigration…Japanese, September 14, 2013.

https://the4forks.wordpress.com/2013/07/09/food-a-universal-language-that-brings-cultures-together/. Food: a universal language that brings cultures together, June 8, 2015.

http://www.yourislandroutes.com/articles/bango.shtml. Lassalle, Melody. The Bango Number System, November 21, 2013.

www.yourdictionary.com/saimin. New World Dictionary, June 28, 2015.

Niiya, Brian. World War II Internment in Hawaii, History of the Internment in Hawaii. 2010. (Resource is no longer available online)

Papers

Higa, Masanori. *The Sociolinguistic Significance of Borrowed Words in the Japanese Spoken in Hawaii.* Honolulu: Hawaii University, Dept. of Linguistics, 1970.

Inoue, Fumio. *A Glossary of Hawaiian Japanese.* March 28, 991, 2nd ed.

Movies

"Nami no Bon" ("Lanterns on Blue Waters"), filmed in Lahaina, Maui, 1983.

Archives and Museums

Bishop Museum

Hawaii Japanese Center (HJC)

Hawaii Plantation Museum

Hawaii's Plantation Village

Japanese Cultural Center of Hawai'i (JCCH)

Japan International Cooperation Agency (JICA)

Lyman House Memorial Museum

North Hawai'i Education and Research Center (NHERC) Heritage Center

Wainaku Ventures (former C. Brewer & Co.)

About the Authors & Illustrator

Myra Sachiko Ikeda was born and raised in Hilo on the Island of Hawai'i during the time when sugar production was considered king and when Hawai'i Plantation Pidgin was her daily interpersonal communication. While the historical, social and linguistic approaches are vital, having the actual experience of using the language as part of her daily life and lifestyle made her realize the importance of the language in the development of Hawai'i.

The natural necessity of communication in order for people to assimilate for their survival and mutual benefit resulted in the development of an intrinsic language. As global communication becomes the norm of today, the knowledge and use of Hawai'i Plantation Pidgin is disappearing as the generations who were born after the immigrant plantation workers became more comfortable with the use of Standard English and Hawai'i Creole English. Hawai'i Plantation Pidgin influenced much of the early years of plantation life. Ikeda believes that this vital part of Hawai'i history needs to be documented.

Ikeda received a Bachelor of Arts Degree in Speech-English and Japanese Studies from the University of Hawai'i at Hilo in 1978. It was while in college that her mother's honor and celebration of the culture, traditions and language of Japan impressed upon her the need to share the history and transformation of the language. It was because of her mother's inspiration that she began the journey to speak with others who also used it as their daily communication and recorded the results on paper.

While serving as the Manager of Administration for the Hawaiʻi Island Economic Development Board from 1995-1999, she assisted with the Rural Economic Transition Assistance-Hawaiʻi (RETA-H) Program sponsored by Senator Daniel Inouye's office. The RETA-H Program provided funds for the transition of sugar cane plantation workers to become entrepreneurs due to the closing of sugar plantations in Hawaiʻi. For Ikeda, this work experience was a stark reminder of the ending era of sugar plantation days and reinforced for her the need to preserve the language used and to recognize its role in the history and culture of Hawaiʻi.

Writer, editor, curator and media consultant **Arnold Hiura** and his wife, Eloise, are partners in MBFT Media, which provides communications services to local companies and community organizations. He previously served as editor of *The Hawaii Herald: A Japanese American Journal,* and as curator with the Japanese American National Museum in Los Angeles.

A few years ago, Arnold and Eloise moved from Honolulu to the plantation town of Papaikou on the Big Island where he was born and raised. They currently serve as executive director and executive assistant, respectively, at the Hawaii Japanese Center in Hilo.

Jeffery Kalehuakea De Costa grew up in the Wainaku district of Hilo on Hawaiʻi Island in a community of former sugar cane workers and their old plantation homes. He spent many hours exploring the nooks and crannies of his playground, the remains of the former Hilo Sugar Mill. His love of drawing was inspired by his desire to capture a moment so that he could remember it always.